Go

GOD–
His and Hers

Elisabeth Moltmann-Wendel
and
Jürgen Moltmann

SCM PRESS

231

Translated by John Bowden from the German
Als Frau und Mann von Gott reden,
published 1991 by Christian Kaiser Verlag.

© Christian Kaiser Verlag 1991

Translation © John Bowden 1991

British Library Cataloguing in Publication Data

Moltmann-Wendel, Elisabeth
  God : his and hers.
  I. Title II. Moltmann, Jürgen
  III. [Als frau und Mann von Gott reden. *English*]
  231

  ISBN 0 334 02017 4

20028560

First British edition published 1991
by SCM Press Ltd,
26-30 Tottenham Road, London N1 4BZ

Phototypeset by Intype, London
and printed in Great Britain by
Billing & Sons Ltd, Worcester

For our friends
Ruth and Karl Lehner

Contents

Introduction

On various occasions in recent years we have constantly been asked to say something about the church, God, and the Bible from both a feminine *and* a masculine perspective. The occasions were very different: ecumenical conferences, a televised church service, reflections on the theology of the cross arising out of our discussions at home. We have put these texts together in the order in which they were written. They also show how we have developed, together and differently. But above all they are meant to show that Christian faith is not a monolith, but can be rich and many-sided.

However, must not some people feel that for women and men now to want to talk again differently about God is to lapse into old gender-related roles? We think that it at this stage we have to think about the *processes* which make us women and men. And these processes are also reflected in spirituality and theology.

Women have proved themselves in all professions and spheres of public life. They are showing that they are not embodiments of nature, conceding the spirit as a male preserve. But it is also becoming increasingly clear that women have different perspectives from men, which are grounded less in biology than in their social experiences. The difference between the sexes is governed not so much by the differences between their bodies as by the different social relationships and insights that result from them – though sometimes these *are* conditioned by the body. But that means that we have to begin neither from biologisms nor from eternal modes of being (ontological categories), but from the historical experiences of women and men as they can be found today in analyses by social psychologists and personal statements.

Some contemporary research shows that this can begin at a very early stage. Most boys have different experiences in early childhood from most girls. The boy learns that he is not like his origin, and this early experience can also be a reason why he is readily prepared to think in dualistic terms: man *or* woman, understanding *or* feeling, brain *or* heart, technology *or* nature, God *or* the world. Nowadays many women, in particular, find these dualisms threatening. Such dualisms mould our thought-patterns, mould us all, mould our world which is predominantly shaped by men. These dualisms are not simply polarities which are part of the fruitful tensions of life. They give the world a hierarchical order, so that men count more than women, understanding must dominate over feeling, and technology is more important than nature. They split the world into a variety of spheres which have nothing to do with one another or grossly contradict one another – a development which is encouraged by industrial and technological progress. Individuals, too, are similarly split, and it becomes increasingly difficult to arrive at any totalities in life.

If we look more closely once again at the way in which boys become persons, we see that in a society fixated on male descendants 'the gleam in the mother's eye' and the high expectations of the family fall on the son. That makes him self-centred and aware of himself. In order to live up to male society and become autonomous, however, the son must soon repress the spheres of feeling, of the mother, of the feminine, and learn rational modes of behaviour controlled by the will. This produces capacities like mastery, concentration, a love of discussion. But there are also shadow-sides: in doing this the male establishes domination in himself. So throughout life the male sex is characterized by the search for certainty, independence and control, the attitude of self-control and domination, though this can also lead to the domination of women and subjects. The spheres of love, care and feeling are thus put at a lower psychological and social level. Behind the mask of a strong man there often lurks uncertainty about feelings and about women and their sphere of life and work, which is compensated for by strength and conceptuality. Will and understanding become the instruments for holding together the fragile male personality. Dogmas and conceptions, once learned, can become the indispensable equipment and also the weapons with which an established entity (church, theology, faith) is defended.

Women have different early experiences, being of the same sex as their mothers. They do not have the same problems of detaching themselves from their mothers and the feminine sphere unless they copy male socialization at a later stage. All their lives they often remain tied to the traditional feminine spheres of care, feeling and relationship, and at the same time they are also continually threatened with being swallowed up by these spheres. Their development towards autonomy is often difficult and creates guilt feelings. In normal women's lives, relationships and help for neighbours always have priority over autonomy. But autonomy can easily be lost in relationships. The problem of many women nowadays is that they often find themselves torn into many pieces by family, work and public responsibilities, yet nevertheless do not give up the system of relationships which is important for all life on this earth, and want to develop an autonomy which does not simply copy male autonomy. It is important for them today to develop self-awareness and a responsibility for themselves which presuppose a degree of self-love.

Women often develop a different view of the world as a result of their socialization. They often take interconnected thought for granted. In pregnancies they have the experience that life in relationships precedes independent life, while in males there is often the opposite pattern of ideas, that individual thought precedes social life. Women are more strongly tied to the material and the social than are men. Their attention is often attracted by something which is apparently unimportant. They do not have stronger feelings than men, but they are accustomed to dealing with their feelings more openly. Women in particular can already experience and are nowadays fully aware of what is emerging as a general insight, that human beings understand with their bodies, grasp with their senses and learn to see though their social experiences.

It follows from this that feminine thought often seems less direct and consistent, but instead grasps reality in a more complex way. Women guard against separating logic and feeling, just as they must also combine manual work and intellectual work, coping with a home and a job. For them, to think with feeling and to feel thoughtfully is now a legitimate task – often difficult, but promising. Both women and men should learn much that is new by thinking in terms of differences (distinctions) rather than mutually exclusive opposites.

Today we are also rediscovering differentiated perspectives in our theological traditions. Granted there is no such thing as a masculine faith or a feminine faith, but there are different patterns of thought, e.g. in understanding salvation, sin or love. They develop from our socialization. They are also moulded by the phases of our life. In her understanding of love, a woman student will perhaps differ from a mother involved with a family in the aspects of love that she stresses. Men, too, can rediscover part of their own identity in women's perspectives, whereas there are still many women who will rediscover themselves best in the images shaped by traditional theology. What is important nowadays, though, is to give expression to those who for so long have remained silent and with them to rediscover the variety and riches of Christian traditions, many of which are unfamiliar.

It is important nowadays to develop openness for such processes. However, time and again a pastor will seem to a laywoman to be no more than the embodiment of power because of his manner of thinking and his theological and dogmatic knowledge. In turn the laywoman will seem to him to be an example of the irrationality and enthusiasm that he has learned to fight against. So far women have had little chance of contributing their patterns of life and thought. The urgent task in all spheres, that of perceiving life and processes in life with sensitivity, calls for the extension of such patterns, which arises above all out of women's lives. It calls for the rethinking and withdrawal of the prevailing, dominant thought.

The two of us are certainly not a typical man and woman, husband and wife, who correspond to the processes of socialization set out here. Indeed there is no such thing as this typical man and typical woman. But those who are sensitive to themselves and others will also constantly feel how much we are all moulded by our social experiences as mother or father, by jobs, looking after a home or by our own social contacts.

A process of new thought, related to life, is taking place today in feminist theology. Unfortunately, in many circles in the church and theology, feminist theology is still feared because it seems to conjure up images of 'man' or 'patriarchy' as enemies. There is no doubt that in fact in some instances there is reason for this fear. We therefore feel it all the more important to point out differences between women and men which are not to be seen as oppositions. Dualistic thought – thinking in exclusive opposites – has a fatal tradition in Christianity. It is still difficult for us to perceive the wealth of distinctions and differences, because the certainty of faith usually thinks that it has to entrench itself behind rigid dogmas. Nor is feminist theology by any means free of absolutist claims. That makes us feel it all the more necessary to turn the distinctive approach of feminism into an interconnected way of thinking and to take cautious steps towards a dialogue which takes our differences seriously. The power of patriarchal structures which women keep experiencing in the church and theology will not be removed by that alone. But it can be made more evident, and the painful way to justice in the church and society can be straightened out. The reciprocal recognition of human justice and human dignity in the structures of the church and also in theological statements will ultimately be the only basis on which the church can become a community of women and men.

Elisabeth Moltmann-Wendel and Jürgen Moltmann

God – His and Hers

1

Becoming Persons in a New Community of Women and Men

The joint opening lecture at an ecumenical conference on
'The Community of Women and Men in the Church',
Sheffield, England, 11-18 July 1981

I

Elisabeth: Church history begins with a small group of women
setting out to perform a last loving service for their dead friend
Jesus. It begins with a small group of women, against all reason
and against all hope, showing their support for a traitor to the
state and doing what they think to be right. What they do has the
quality of life: they love a life which has been given up, and never
give up what is dead. It begins with Jesus meeting them, greeting
them, allowing himself to be touched by them as he has touched
them in their lives and raised them up. And it begins with the
women having to communicate to men this experience, this life,
which they have understood and grasped with their hands.

This story, as Matthew tells it, is known to everyone as the
story of the women at the tomb, but not as the beginning of church
history. Church history begins officially with the sending out of
the male apostles, and officially these do not include any women.
To the present day, many churches derive themselves from this
apostolic succession. Almost all of them are governed by men,
have been moulded by men and are sustained by male notions.
God is thought of in predominantly masculine terms. What he
does has been orientated on male leadership roles: he controls,
judges, rules; and what he is accords with male desires: he is
judge, king, ruler, warlord. The experiences of women, that Jesus
is a friend who shares their life, who gives warmth, nearness,
tenderness to all who are forsaken and helpless, are forgotten
here. Feminism, the women's movement of the Western world,

has given many women the courage to discover themselves, to express again their own experiences of God, to read the Bible with new eyes, and to rediscover their original and unique role in the gospel. For them feminism is no white, Western, middle-class movement, but is deeply grounded in the gospel.

In the social upheavals and cultural crises of the last fifteen years, many other groups have had the painful experience that God is to be found on the side of patriarchy. God has become alien, above all, to many women from the Western world. He can no longer be reconciled with their conceptions and their identity. However, patriarchy is not something which is the fault of the male. Men should not feel personally responsible for it. Patriarchy is a thousand-year-old cultural form. without which many of the cultural and economic achievements of our world would be unthinkable. But particularly over the last two centuries it has led to pernicious links with colonialism and racism, capitalism and sexism, so that we have begun to look for the basic cause of this evil. And here it has become terrifyingly clear to us that a patriarchal Christianity has supported, legitimated and given a religious overtone to colonialism, capitalism, racism and sexism. 'God with us' was written on German belt-buckles in the First World War. People were made slaves, workers were exploited and women brought up to be silent in the name of a triumphal God who was to improve the world. And only marginal groups of Christians have protested against this.

Today women are again on the way towards discovering life, raising the dead to life again, understanding Jesus as the one who he once was for them. They want to get out of the patriarchal domination in which thinking was done *for* them and for others who allegedly had not come of age. They want to escape from the supervision which allowed them to make only a much reduced contribution to the discussion, if it allowed them any voice at all. They are no longer willing to recognize the values communicated by the patriarchal world order – for themselves, for their children, or for society as a whole.

What do women want?

I would like to go into that briefly, since particularly in the church there is also much anxiety about women: anxiety among men that women hate them; anxiety among women about women who are making them feel insecure in their old role. There is anxiety about any kind of radicalism, which is supposed to be incompatible with the love of Christ. What women want is a new society in which the powerful begin to listen to the powerless, in which the powerless have possibilities of expressing and organizing themselves. They want a society in which power is shared round and in which people learn to renounce power – for the sake of justice. They want a society which is not exclusively orientated on the idea of profit and the growth of the economy, but on the needs of *all* people. And they can legitimately and passionately advocate this because they have experienced in their own bodies what it means to be taken charge of, to be kept under control, to be deprived of rights, to live life at second-hand (a man's hand), to give life – but only in a narrow domestic circle, not to shape it in society. We want a total life which embraces body, soul and spirit, a life which is no longer divided into private and public spheres, and which fills us with trust and hope beyond biological death.

This seems to be a great, impossible, utopian programme. But in the end it is no more than the implementation of what can be read in the visions of peace in the prophet Isaiah and something of what the apostle Paul once recognized in a flash: that in Christ there are no Jews, no Greeks, no slaves nor free people, no male and no female. And it is the old vision of women which emerges in one of the oldest passages in the Bible, the song of Miriam: trust in God, who has thrown horse and rider – nowadays we could say sex and domination – into the sea. This women's tradition, which occurs in many women's songs, with Hannah, Deborah, Judith and Mary, is still with us today; it sharpens our hearing of what is going on in the world and what is taking place in ourselves, in our bodies, our souls and our spirits.

Women on the way towards discovering life;
Women in a church which is firmly in male hands;
Where does the way lead?

Certainly it leads away from patriarchy, which has oppressed women, stopped their lips and kept them under control.

But does it also lead away from the church and its patriarchal structures?

Does it also lead away from God, who – as Kate Millet has said

– was always on the side of patriarchy, or – as it might be put better – was always occupied by patriarchy? For many women, even among us, this decision has not yet been made.

Jürgen: You ask whether God is on the side of patriarchy. I would like to attempt an answer by asking myself self-critically: Which God is the God of patriarchy?

Patriarchy did not come into the world through Christianity. It is an old, widespread, male ruling order. Christianity could not get the better of it. Rather, at a very early stage the church was taken over by men and used to advance patriarchy. As a result the liberating potential of Christianity was paralysed. That was detected in other contexts by theologians of hope, liberation theologians and political theologians, in their criticisms of the Constantinian captivity of the church. It has now been shown up completely by feminist theology. So the liberation of women, and subsequently also men, from patriarchy is connected with a rediscovery of the freedom of Jesus and a new experience of the energies of the Spirit. We shall leave behind us the monotheistic God of lords and males and discover from the origins of Christianity the God of community, who is rich in relationships, capable of suffering, and brings about unity. That is the living God, the God of life, whom patriarchy has distorted by the idols of domination. In him males, too, will experience liberation from the distortions that they themselves have suffered and still suffer as a result of patriarchy.

Of course oppression has two sides: the master on one, the slave on the other; here the man who rules and there the woman who serves. Oppression destroys humanity on both sides: the oppressed are robbed of their humanity and the oppressors become inhuman. Both experience alienation from their true being, but with the difference that one suffers as a result of this, whereas the other seems to feel quite content about it. The liberation from oppression must take place on both sides. How is that possible for men, whose feelings and ideas are moulded by patriarchy and who enjoy its privileges?

I think that for us men, as for you women, it begins by our becoming aware of our real situation and recognizing how much patriarchy cheats us of the happiness of true life. Any man can work this out for himself by asking what feelings he had to learn to suppress, what drives he had to learn to control, and what roles he had to study, when as a child he was brought up to be 'a man'. He was brought up to be a worker, a soldier, a wage-earner, father of a family, to conquer and to rule. So the first thing he learned was self-control and self-mastery. And as a result he constantly became anxious that he was a 'nothing' and had to 'make something of himself'.

Patriarchy has halved the male. It has split him into a subject with reason and will, with which he has to identify, and an object with a heart, feeling and needs, from which he has to distance himself. In so doing it has isolated the male and to some degree made him hate himself. This division of the male is also reflected in the masculine subjection and domination of the supposedly 'weak', 'emotional', 'physical' woman, and turns into aggression. It is also reflected on the other side: any ruler needs not only subjects which he can dominate but also a throne on which he can sit. The throne on which the ruling male sits is the mother, as can be seen in the case of Isis-Horus, Mary and the child Jesus, and other symbols. This splitting of the woman into mother and wife is a product of patriarchy. Unresolved ties to the mother and *machismo* towards other women go together. Mothering and domination must cease at the same time, otherwise men will be neither free nor mature.

The God of patriarchy reflects in his greatness the misery of the halved and isolated male: he is the Omnipotent, the Lord, the Absolute. He determines everything, and nothing influences him. He is incapable of suffering. According to Aristotle he loves only himself and moves everything to join in his self-love. If he is given human features, then these are male. To know him, one goes up from the father of the family to the father of the people, from the father of the people to the church father, and gets to the Father of All in heaven. One then descends again from the heavenly Father to provide legitimation for authorities. This Father of All in heaven has nothing to do with Jesus's 'Abba' mystery. Rather, he came into being from the first division of the world into heaven and earth: Heavenly Father and Mother Earth.

In Christian forms the God of patriarchy tends to be thought of in corporate terms. The man is the head of the woman, Christ is the head of the man, God is the head of Christ (I Cor.11.3). Only under the man as head is the woman then the image of God (I Cor.11.7): theologians like Augustine and Thomas Aquinas say that she is not the image of God in her own right. Karl Barth says that the superiority of the male is a reference to the superiority of God.

The wretchedness of the male ruler-God lies in the fact that he has no name and is solitary. He is defined only by his function as ruler and possessor of the world. Who he himself is remains unknown. So God is halved, separated and isolated, by patriarchy. But a God who is only 'The Almighty' is not God, but a monster. The man who emulates this God becomes an unhappy beast; he consists only of the will to power. Since this 'God complex', as H.E.Richter calls it, has befallen modern, white man, patriarchy no longer produces order but destruction, no longer leads to preservation but to anxiety.

You said that women today are on the way towards discovering life, full life in community. Men who want to discover life for themselves and then in community with women must shake off the pressure of patriarchy as a nightmare and do away with these repressions of true life in order to be complete persons. Here we are probably like the disciples who heard the women's Easter message and then set off, believing yet not believing, to find for themselves the Living One whom they had forsaken on his cross before his death. In the whole resurrection movement we men could discover 'the new community of men and women' which redeems us from patriarchal distortions and opens us up to full human life.

II

Elisabeth: Both men and women are deformed, but in different ways and with different consequences. The throne of Isis has been preserved for you, even if we no longer want to be the mothers who support it.

So today women should go forward on the way to a new community of women and men. That is not necessary primarily in order to make good the discrimination and injustice that women have experienced. Nor should it bring humiliation to men. Rather, it should be the opportunity to find room for women to bring to awareness and to express the obstacles on this way. For only in this way can a new sustainable community grow.

Since we have begun to discover what *our* life is, our life as women, our life in solidarity with all women who are discriminated against all over the world, our spiritual life, our life as Christians, life which we want to grasp, trace, experience, change, we have kept coming up against the barrier of our Christian tradition. Our faith is the faith of the 'fathers'; our testimonies of faith come from a Bible which has been put together in a patriarchal way, evidently without any women being involved. Our hymns sing of Christian life from the perspective of the father of the household. In our theology, as Karl Barth put it, the man 'leads' and the woman 'is led'. And if we look more closely, then the tradition by which we are asked to live is a treasure-trove of misogynism. At all events the life which is intended for us by this tradition is not a whole life. According to one passage in the Bible *we* are to be saved by bearing children, and *you* by faith. We are to keep silent; you may speak. We led you astray and were the first to sin. But even if one overlooks these biblical *faux pas*, ours is a life at second hand, life as a supplement to the man, life from the spirit and the word, but not from the unity of body, soul and spirit. For too long in the patriarchal tradition our bodies have been regarded as embarrassing, impure and offensive. That is not the fullness of life, but a halved life.

Can the Christian tradition help us out of our halved life? Where do we find sources and motivations for our identity? What Christian traditions can guide us on the way to wholeness? What Christian traditions can also help men to be 'whole' and give them a different identity from that of the patriarch?

Jürgen: The biblical, Christian and church traditions were indeed primarily written and put together by dominant males. So at first sight they do not offer much for the liberation of women. History, it has been said, is always 'written by the victors'. The losers are robbed even of the awareness of their own history of humiliation and suffering. Now we can read these traditions 'from above', but we can also read them – contrary to the way in which they were intended – 'from below'. If we do, we will also find in the stories of the rulers the repressed histories of rebellions against their rule. In this sense there is also a Christian history of women in and under male church history. You yourself have rediscovered part of this and have found in it symbols and motives which can emerge from a halved life and lead to a whole life. But here and there one can also find stories of freedom in the male history. I would like to call attention to three of them.

1. For thousands of years all Christians have learned the story of the Fall according to the second account of creation. It is very vivid. It also contains the first male excuse: 'The woman whom you gave to be with me gave me of the fruit of the tree' (Gen.3.12). Moreover, this also occurs in the New Testament. 'For Adam was formed first, then Eve; and Adam was not deceived, but the woman was deceived and became a transgressor' (I Tim.2.13f.). That is given as the reason for the inferiority of women. By comparison, the story of the Fall according to the first account of creation, the Priestly Writing, is completely forgotten. Here there is no mention of fruit, woman, serpent and Adam (who is innocent and stupid); we have something else. 'Now the earth was corrupt in God's sight, and the earth was filled with evil' (Gen.6.11-13). What was this evil? It consisted in the spread of 'acts of violence' among human beings and animals. Therefore God resolved to destroy both through the flood. Here evil, sin at its origin, is none other than 'acts of violence', the use of force. So redemption consists of a 'non-violent life' of the kind that Jesus called for and promised in the Sermon on the Mount. Had we paid better attention to this story, we would never have arrived at the myth of the inferiority of the woman.

2. Women today ask critically, 'Is God a "man"?' The Christian doctrine of God does in fact seem to present predominantly masculine persons: Father – Son – Holy Spirit. But is that really the case? There is an old, suppressed tradition of the motherhood of the Holy Spirit. The Christian communities which were later excluded from the mainstream, male, church as 'Gnostics' were able to speak of the Spirit as the mother of Jesus and mother of the reborn. Ethiopian icons of the Trinity show the Spirit as mother. And the Greek church fathers often saw the nuclear family – Adam, Eve and Seth – as the image of the triune God,

which presupposes that the Holy Spirit is feminine and is the primal image of the mother. It was probably not by chance that Count Zinzendorf rediscovered the motherhood of the Spirit when founding the community of brothers and sisters in Pennsylvania in 1741: 'That is the divine family on earth, as the Father of our Lord Jesus Christ is our true father, the Spirit of our Lord Jesus Christ is our true mother, because the Son of the living God is our true brother.' I find this notion helpful, not only because it discovers the feminine principle in the Godhead, but also because it accepts an element of truth in panentheism. If the Spirit is our mother, then I feel not only 'under God' but also 'in God'. The notion frees me from one-sided, monotheistic images of the father and helps me to experience the whole God with the whole of my being. It helps me to find in our community the God who is community.

3. Finally, I discover that the development of the doctrine of the Trinity in the Christian concept of God, difficult and abstract though it is, has already prepared for a superseding of the male Lord God. Certainly, in terms of an abstract male theology, 'Trinity' has connotations of being 'from above'. But I think that it indicates the mystery of the totality, which embraces our whole and common life. Knowledge of God and knowledge of self always have an effect on each other. The theology of the Western church saw the image of God in human beings as the fact that they have 'souls endowed with reason' which control their bodies. In their lordship over themselves and the earth, human beings – i.e. men – correspond to the Lord God. An individualistic understanding of human beings and a monotheistic understanding of God arose together. If we now recognize that human beings form a unity of body, soul and spirit, and find their salvation in the experience of the totality of life, then the image of God on earth cannot just be their souls. In their bodily nature, in the community of women and men, they correspond to God. But which God? Surely the God who is rich in relationships, who unites, who forms community, in short the triune God. This God does not rule by dividing and isolating ('divide and rule'), but is present in the union of what is separated and the healing of what is divided. The poweful male may be an imitation of the Almighty, but only a human community can be the image of the triune God,

a community in which people have everything in common, apart from their personal characteristics, and share it. This idea helps me to seek God not only above, in heaven, nor only deep within my soul, but above all *among us* in our community.

'What helps us out of our halved life?' you asked. What Christian traditions can guide us on the way to totality? Past hopes and past experiences are constantly stored up in our traditions. That has value, but only limited value. No tradition can lay down the future. At best, traditions can prepare the way for the future. The Spirit itself constantly creates new things and is full of surprises. The Spirit is not bound to traditions, but takes from them whatever points towards the future. Christianity is more than a tradition; it is a hope.

Elisabeth: It will continue to be difficult for many women to rediscover themselves in the feminine correlations to male conceptions of God. Their question is: Can we rediscover our identity in masculine symbols – supplemented by feminine imaginings?

They will trust their own fantasies more than tradition. Now they are already developing their own language: God is the baker's wife. Jesus can be their sister. They pray, 'Our Father/ Mother in heaven'. For many women, feminist theology – and the very mention of the term sends shivers down the backs of many theologians – is the only possible way of loosening their tongues and showing that they are daughters of God. Women have a culture of their own. It is different again in the different countries in Asia, in Africa. It is more concrete, more full of images than the corresponding male culture, but it has often been buried. So for us theology has been supplemented by theo-fantasy, which reopens the buried sources.

It will be important for theology – which is predominantly a male preserve – to take seriously not only past experiences and traditions but also present experiences and those to come: theo-fantasy. Life – including Christian life – is more colourful and complex than a written tradition. Here it will be important for men to learn to listen and sit at the feet of women – as Mary sat at Jesus' feet.

Elisabeth: A new community can mature and become fruitful only if women remain their own persons. Only if their singularity, their special character, their uniqueness are preserved can the contribution that they make to society remain alive. Only if they continue to make *their* concern the life that they lack and have now discovered, can it be the common concern of all.

To many people, men and also women, that sour.ds harsh and paradoxical. We are accustomed to seeing the church as the great community of love, where one person holds back for the sake of another, where people forget themselves for the sake of a great cause. A great 'we' should bind everyone and everything together.

If women and men want to come together to form a new community, they must say good-bye to these daydreams. They must accept the pain of separation and also the possible loss of love, each for herself or himself. They can discover themselves – in their totality with all its undisclosed possibilities.

This may sound particularly hard to some women in the church, since they are used to giving themselves up, or quickly holding back, and many have internalized this as their Christian lifestyle. It is hard for men, since they are used to collaborating with women who are always ready to love, and by virtue of their ministries and the power in the churches attached to them they have made the cause of Jesus a patriarchy of love. We must learn to love anew, with a love which helps others to come of age, does not oppress them and does not exalt them, a love which opens up a sphere that is free of domination.

The responsibility which men are accustomed to take and the sacrifices which women are accustomed to make are patterns of behaviour which have emerged from a strict division of roles between the sexes. They are patriarchal modes of behaviour by which our churches live, but no new community can grow from them today. Women have begun to detach themselves from their role. How can men do the same?

Jürgen: I think that I should move on further before I get to the question of the church. To begin with, women who are liberating themselves from age-old subjection make men feel insecure.

Women should not conceal this out of love and men should not deny it out of arrogance. We are becoming insecure in the male roles which are assigned to us. We have to relearn them, and all existential relearning involves pain. But it goes even deeper. Men also feel wounded in their male pride. Their feeling of worth is shattered. Their patriarchal identity falls apart. They can react to that with aggression, but mostly they react to it with depression.

Women are experiencing their new identity, their dignity and their liberation to full humanity. Men are finding it difficult to follow them, because first they have to return far back into themselves, to discover the starting point for their own liberation to full humanity. They have to break through the shell of their alienation to arrive at the kernel of their human nature. Here they have to give up male self-righteousness in order to learn to trust in their humanity. To put it simply: the master in the man has to die in order to make possible the birth of the brother who is ready for open friendship.

For men, too, that means that they can no longer identify themselves with the male caste but must break out of the male codex. They will be despised for that. They may become lonely. The male caste has always played the strongest part in bringing up the child to be a 'man'. It also punishes dissidents as 'traitors'.

Anyone who is ready to renounce the male privileges which the patriarchal society gives him must also learn to take back his male responsibility for the so-called 'weaker sex'. Many of us find it particularly difficult to give up this morality, because it makes one so 'noble', so 'chivalrous' and 'gentlemanlike'. But any man who welcomes and recognizes that women have come of age must also take back his responsibility.

IV

Elisabeth: Are the churches, which sometimes seem to me to be such male alliances, strong enough to tolerate the fact that so many of us who have been kept under are now coming of age? Are they ready to take seriously the rights of women who are nowadays discovering that they are persons in their own right – and that means giving them these rights and giving them *power*?

There is an explosive danger in this subjectivity, an upsurge of a creativity which has never come to fruition. It affects much that is well-tried in the church. It puts in question images of God and forms of life. 'We are the church,' some women are saying today. Does their way lead to a new community of men and women?

Jürgen: The Christian church finds the limitation of responsibility particularly difficult, because serving, caring for, interceding for others, and thus responsibility, represent the supreme values in it. This gentle dictatorship of love, the 'patriarchy of love' as you call it, is really difficult to avoid. Is not a Christian 'always serving' and always only 'there for others'? I think that that is no longer the case, indeed I think that it is wrong, and a disguised form of a desire to dominate. A Christian is first of all 'there with others'. But Christians can also be 'there for others', if necessary, only if they are ready to live with others. Their love finds its limits in the independence of others. Even Jesus did not come to fetter people by serving them in such a way as to make himself indispensable to them. He always said, 'Your faith has helped you', when people wanted to thank him for healings: your *own* faith! God himself is always there 'for us' only in our need, for he wants to live in eternity 'with us'. He wants us as 'our own people', as you have put it.

Now as long as a church understands itself as a serving church, as a 'church *for* the people' or a 'church *for* the world' or a 'church *for* others', it will always see the subjectivity and the coming of age of the objects of which it takes charge as a danger to itself. Only if this church which takes charge 'from above' becomes the community of the people will it welcome in their own right, as subjects, women, workers, the handicapped, and see them as powers of the Spirit. In the established churches few women are pastors and even fewer are bishops. However, in many Latin American base communities the leadership of women is taken for granted. So far, only once-persecuted communities and base communities have experienced the fullness of the charisms in the free community of men and women, a community without any 'above' and 'below'. For the old male church, the liberating Spirit will, paradoxically, in all probability, come 'from below'. We should look for it where men and women take charge of their own lives and embark on initiatives of their own.

V

Elisabeth: The power which is now bringing women to life in the face of patriarchal structures, in the face of their own uncertainty and lack of courage, which is making them free to stand upright like the woman who was bent over, and who was healed by Jesus, which is making them discover sisters, is the power of the Holy Spirit. For many people, for a long time, this Spirit was miraculous. But many people are finding in the Spirit the means of identification which the male church, the male God, the man Jesus could not give them. They speak of the Holy Spirit as she – and in the language of Jesus the Spirit actually was feminine in gender. Nor are they the first people to be doing this. In the long history of the patriarchal church, women were constantly able to break through the ruling structures in the name of the Holy Spirit. But the church always mistrusted them and the Spirit, condemning the working of the Spirit as enthusiasm, heresy, paganism. The Spirit was attached to particular ministries and robbed of its renewing power.

Can we trust the Spirit again today – on the way to a new community? Can we trust the Spirit of enthusiasts, crazy people, outsiders, visionaries, those who have understood and grasped life, like the women on Easter morning, whose reports seemed like fairy tales to the disciples? Can we – against all reason – dare a shared revival in the name of this Spirit? Can we remove the age-old mistrust of women when they do not just speak in a balanced way, rationally and in a male language?

Jürgen: The feminist appeal to the Holy Spirit is difficult for some people to accept because they are not sure whether this is the 'Holy Spirit' or another Spirit. There have always been a variety of charismatic and spiritist communities which were moved by many spirits, but not necessarily just by the divine Spirit. So out of anxiety over the chaos of spirits, at a very early stage the church tied the Holy Spirit to consecration to the office of bishop. In addition, in the Western church the Spirit was tied into the chain of christology by the *filioque*, the Spirit proceeding from the Son as well as from the Father. In that case Spirit is just the subjective activity of Christ, the word and the sacraments of the church. There is no room here for the creative innovation and surprises of the Holy Spirit – not even room for expectation.

In order that we may become open to the surprising new activity of the Spirit, I would like to suggest that we make a clear distinction between the source of the Spirit and the criterion for discerning the spirits. The source of the Spirit is God, and what comes from this source is as colourful and varied as creation itself. Therefore the Christians in the New Testament always talk exuberantly when they are speaking of the fullness, the riches and the inexhaustible character of the Spirit. That is how they have experienced the Spirit. Everyone has more than enough gifts of the Spirit. No one lacks anything. And when the Spirit of God is poured out on 'all flesh', 'the daughters prophesy' (Joel 3.1) also. For the first Christians, the criterion for discerning the diverse spirits was encounter with the crucified Christ. Whatever could stand before the crucified Christ was the divine Spirit. Whatever contradicted the crucified Christ because it was the spirit of power or vanity was rejected. To return to our story at the beginning: How did the women recognize the risen, living Christ? They could have thought that he was a ghost or some other figure. They recognized the risen Christ immediately because they had remained faithful to him, even to his death on the cross. They recognized him immediately by the marks of the nails and the way in which he had lived with them. And the life-giving Spirit is certainly to be recognized in just the same way: that Spirit brings us into the liberating community of Jesus and brings Jesus in a liberating way to us.

Elisabeth: A last question which I find an urgent one is: Why did this women's experience disappear so quickly?

Why did a sustainable community of women and men fail to come into being almost two thousand years ago?

Perhaps it was because of women who trusted social structures more than themselves; who heeded men more than God; who reverted to their old female role and did not put their trust in the renewing power of the resurrection.

In our different countries and different churches we represent the cause of women: some of us are fighting only for survival, others are calling for the right to become pastors or priests. The issues are money, influence, teaching posts, a better social order. We live in different kinds of societies and have different presuppositions.

One thing seems important to me, and I think that we have it in common. We must trust ourselves again and we must trust the renewing power of our experience of God. We must trust ourselves to communicate life with all our senses and capacities and not give way to unyielding structures nor keep on lapsing into false obedience in the face of authorities. We must become ourselves in body, soul and spirit so that this spark leaps over to men, brothers, fathers, mothers and children.

2

Jesus did not talk of appeasement . . .

Men and women; oppressors and oppressed; emancipation and redemption

A conversation with the journal *Publik-Forum*, 1984

Publik-Forum: Frau Moltmann-Wendel, Herr Moltmann, you both teach Protestant theology and have long been concerned with 'liberation theology'. 'Liberation' is also going to be the subject of our conversation. What does 'liberation' mean for you in your theology?

Elisabeth: For me, liberation theology is something quite concrete, not global. Specifically it is the liberation of the woman for herself, for her personality, for her own particular situation. Perhaps the easiest way of making this clear is to quote from a letter which a woman recently wrote to me: 'When I dare to say "I *may*", it's like a prayer.' For me, liberation today is when women discover themselves in this way. That can happen in very different ways: through social actions, through the rediscovery of an inner life, as a new self-discovery. For me, everything that changes in this way is liberation.

Publik-Forum: Did one specific event or experience lead you to discover feminist theology?

Elisabeth: For twenty years I thought that my destiny and my calling was to be a mother and a wife, always to help and fill in, and always to remain unobtrusive in these functions. And then the women's movement suddenly made me aware, above all through the theological grounding that I learned in the United States, that that was not God's purpose for me.

Jürgen: For me liberation theology is rather more traditionally Latin American liberation theology, that theology which was developed in the Third World from the recognition of social and political dependence and the situation of oppression. My question is how this Latin American liberation theology can be transferred to the First World. While Latin America is concerned with the liberation of the *oppressed*, here our concern is with the liberation of the *oppressors*. For where mechanisms of oppression are dominant, there is alienation from the human on both sides. Perhaps we have not yet discovered that properly here.

Publik-Forum: When you talk of the liberation of the oppressor, by that do you also mean the males in the church?

Jürgen: Yes.

Publik-Forum: How can one liberate these males?

Jürgen: To give a traditional answer: through true faith. For if the male has no true faith, he identifies his humanity with his manhood, and draws his feeling of worth from his masculinity. That is a kind of self-justification and self-righteousness which one finds among men everywhere. The rigidity of this identification is, of course, bound up with upbringing. That gives rise to an aggressive identity. A man can only identify himself rightly as a man if he constantly tells himself that he is not a woman and if he can always exercise domination over women. Liberation from this attitude is urgently necessary for men in the church, but also for men outside the church.

Publik-Forum: Your wife has just said that at one point she felt 'That can't be God's plan for me?' What can God's plan be for men? Surely the time has come when men must consider what God's plan is for them?

Jürgen: That's right. I've already indicated that one finds a way out of this cramped masculine identity into a human, open identity; that in this way one develops into a complete human being and gives up this male fixation. That is not a sacrifice, but a gain in humanity.

Elisabeth: That's all very grandiose. I think it means, in a much more modest way, that men have to hold back and no longer stand up for everything; they can't keep talking about everything, but must put themselves in the position of listeners, of accepters. A second consequence, which has yet to be realized in the church, is that men must give back privileges. When we have men giving up a position, honour, respect in favour of women, then for me renewal in the church has begun.

Publik-Forum: Does that mean that as a woman you are

making an appeal to men? For me the question is whether men can or should set this church reform in motion at all. Basically aren't women the active ones, even in the question of male emancipation?

Elisabeth: The psychoanalyst Horst-Eberhard Richter has a theory that women have an advantage in their capacity for suffering and emotion. Women are more sensitive, are more oppressed by suffering and in a better position to express contemporary problems. They also claim to speak for all human beings. It is no coincidence that women have leading positions in civil rights initiatives or in the Green movement. They are simply more on the ball. They feel more strongly and perhaps to a greater degree than men where the shoe pinches.

Jürgen: It is important for us men to give up responsibility. Men always feel responsible for everything, especially in the church. That is really a concealed form of domination. Not to have to feel responsible for everything means standing back, achieving a degree of humanity, so that this male complex, which looks so like the God-complex, simply falls apart.

Publik-Forum: In the church, aren't men really afraid of women? What makes men afraid?

Elisabeth: There is an age-old anxiety about mothers who prove suffocating, and this probably plays a very important role in all these male/female relationships. Men have to try to sever the tie with their mothers, emerge from the intimate sphere of their mothers. They are constantly dogged by this fear of being suffocated by their mothers. This is also part of their socialization: to become strong, to become completely separate from one's mother, an independent male personality. The competition with women brings out these old anxieties again. Good women find it easier to establish themselves. Our woman pastor in the church preached well and was convincing. But the question is much more difficult: what must a male church do to give women, too, opportunities to become 'good' in this way? That's the real problem. It calls for efforts to give up privileges. Only at this point does renewal begin.

Publik-Forum: So are you personally optimistic that this renewal will succeed?

Elisabeth: Yes – with a new, unselfish generation of men, who experience themselves in a new way, who discover all their limitations. We shall never succeed with an infantile, neurotic, childish generation of men.

Publik-Forum: Catholic women say: We want to change the church, we want to change ourselves within the church, but hand in hand with men. I can see difficulties there, since the distance between men above and women below is so very great. Things are rather different in the Protestant church. How long should feminist theology remain feminist before it becomes a shared theology, a theology in partnership?

Elisabeth: Let's take marriage: to think of husband and wife as a close 'we' no longer works. Wife and husband are both individual personalities and they must develop their ideas, including their conception of God and their conception of faith, on the basis of their personalities. When that happens, a two-way dialogue can take place. That, for me, would be partnership. That is also how I see the relationship between feminist and male theology.

Jürgen: I would like to use the word 'friendship' here, since friendship includes attention to the other's freedom and respect for it. This expression is also used in the Gospel of John for the disciples of Jesus, men and women. Friendship is a voluntary tie.

Publik-Forum: We are talking about liberation, liberation theology, emancipation. Is there any difference for you between liberation and emancipation? Or do the two terms now mean the same thing in Christian understanding?

Jürgen: No, liberation goes far wider. Emancipation denoted the freeing of slaves or the freeing of children at eighteen or twenty-one years of age. That is the origin of the term. By contrast, liberation in the economic, political, cultural and religious sphere is a more comprehensive term, which can have a whole series of new connotations. If we begin with economic liberation we immediately see that this also includes motivating people who have become so apathetic and miserable that they no longer have any confidence whatsoever in themselves. Their self-confidence must be strengthened before any economic liberation is conceivable. I find the term liberation fruitful because it is open in a forward direction.

Publik-Forum: There is also the theological term redemption.

It is constantly said that 'liberation' is too one-sided, too this-worldly, and reduces Christian truth. What do you say to that?

Jürgen: I think that Latin American liberation theology sees the two together but does not identify them. Redemption for new, eternal life happens now, already, in this liberation or that. So the old division into two spheres is abandoned but not reduced. The speech which Pope John Paul II made in Nicaragua, in which he said that priests should not take part in the liberation of the people but prepare men and women for eternal life, is still stamped by this old dualism. That is a false alternative. Liberation theologians have long got past it. They do not reduce redemption to a socio-economic liberation, though they are constantly accused of that, but see that redemption already begins in social and economic liberation. And in doing this they have chosen the same basic theological option that we chose with political theology in Europe, which also sees the one in the other.

Publik-Forum: So what could liberation theology specifically mean for me as a Christian, a woman Christian in this country?

Elisabeth: First of all, for me it means that I also relate Christian redemption to the whole social situation, for example that of women. Liberation is this extension of inwardness outwards, so that we no longer understand our whole existence from within, outwards, but in everything, including the external relationships in which we live. Here in Europe there are no longer class struggles, but there are many other kinds of oppression, for example of a psychological or a family kind: we have quite different dreams, visions of liberation, from, for example, those of the Latin Americans.

Jürgen: Specifically, for me liberation means solidarity and community with those at whose expense we live.

Publik-Forum: What would be the *political* element within this liberation, particularly against the background of this somewhat apocalyptic age?

Jürgen: The first point would be liberation from the system of nuclear deterrence which is now consuming all our resources and is calling for unprecedented sacrifice from victims in the Third World. The second would be liberation from the economic system of injustice in world society, because by the simple calculations of experts that costs the lives of thirty million people a year. The inferno is not just a threat in the future, but has already begun among the weakest of the weak. Children are dying in masses in the Third World, people are starving, not because of natural catastrophes or because they cannot help themselves, but because of the injustices of the world economic system. The system of nuclear deterrence and the unjust ordering of the world economy are at present the motive forces of the apocalyse. Unless we dismount from these two horses of the apocalyse we shall see first the weak dying, and then ourselves.

Publik-Forum: So what would be the task of political theology in this context?

Jürgen: Almost all the churches are agreed that the apartheid system of white racism is sin and leads to the *status confessionis*. In other words, you can only say 'No' to the apartheid system in Africa. Whether you believe or not is related to your attitude to apartheid. Apartheid is not a political issue which needs merely to be assessed. That is clearly the case in the Lutheran World Federation, the Reformed World Alliance and the Catholic Church. Thus consensus has been achieved on a broad front. You cannot be involved in apartheid as a Christian; here you have to say No.

The next point is that some churches, namely the Reformed Churches in Holland and in West Germany, have said that the system of nuclear deterrence is a *status confessionis*. To say No to the system of nuclear deterrence is to confess Christ, and to say Yes is to deny him. That is the supreme emergency brake that one can put on in the church. In a few years all the great confessions will arrive at the insight that the system of nuclear deterrence is a sin and thus anti-Christian, and they will proclaim the *status confessionis* on this question. That will mean that if soldiers still support this system of nuclear deterrence they can no longer be in a state of salvation, as Luther asserted to the 'warriors' of his time.

The third step would be also to proclaim the *status confessionis* in respect of the unjust world economic system. That will be very difficult, because the counter-strategies of big businesses can already be detected, for example in suppressing Latin American liberation theology, which is already active on this point. So these would be the three great problem areas where the *status confessionis* must be proclaimed in a situation which looks very apocalyptic.

Publik-Forum: At the same time that means that theology first speaks in very concrete terms, that it addresses very specific areas, and that it also *evaluates*, in a negative sense. Does it follow from this that there are conflicts, disputes, and that here in practice theologians are pioneers?

Jürgen: I would not speak of theologians as pioneers. Most tend to lag behind somewhat and reflect on where others have already gone ahead. There are groups which take initiatives, peace or Third World groups, which have gone ahead here and which the theologians then follow. In the discussion on peace, the Reformed Church in West Germany to which I belong first wrote a letter to all the local churches and took the answers into account; then it came to a decision. The condemnation of the nuclear deterrent was thus not thought up from above or by particularly progressive theologians, but arose from the grass roots.

Publik-Forum: But this very decision has sparked off a basic conflict in the church. If one looks at such questions and identifies very specifically what needs to be changed, does that mean the end of peace in the church?

Jürgen: Yes. The truth of the gospel is also expressed more in conflict than in general appeasement. At any rate, Jesus did not talk of appeasement.

Publik-Forum: There are various forms of liberation theology. If we look at them against the background of an increasing secularization, an increasing dissociation of people from the church, the question arises whether living out liberation theology on a wide scale can bring religion, Christianity and the church rather nearer to people.

Elisabeth: I think that Sunday church Christianity is coming to an end. We shall get new forms of Christianity. One can already experience new beginnings at church rallies, conferences and elsewhere. But we must bring such possibilities to life locally to a much greater extent, in the communities, and there remint the great forms of Christian living in small coins and make it possible for everyone to experience them.

Jürgen: The question really needs to be put the other way round. Does liberation theology help the church to come closer to the people and become the church of Christ? To that I think that one can answer 'Yes'. It does not bring people to church but the church to people, so that a new form of Christianity is coming to life in the many discipleship groups: here we no longer have Christianity as a religion which is alienated, but Christianity for the kingdom of God.

3

Our Image of God

God as Father

Elisabeth Moltmann-Wendel

In recent years many Christian women and men have made efforts to rediscover God as mother. In male circles it was almost tabu to speak of God the Father. Women discovered so many other names and images for God, in the Bible and in tradition and outside them, that the Father retreated into the shadows and was often only a shadow, the dark side of God. I myself do not want to give up the Father God, but for me, too, at first he was banished to a niche at the side, and I think that it it is a good thing that that happened. So for me the invitation to write about my image of God as Father is a return to the past, indeed even more, a return to childhood. I have to ask myself how God became Father for me, and then have to go on to ask whether and how this father image is still important for me.

For me, God who loves me, frees me, makes me independent, was always associated with the name Father. God – the Father – goes deep into the roots of my own experience of a father. And in recent years that seems to have become clear for most people: we can no longer put God in heaven and separate him from our personal experiences. We experience God in our experiences with people around us. My father died early, when I was eight years old. The two years during which he had a serious heart complaint and my mother was anxiously torn between her husband and the children must be left out of this time of experience. A few images keep recurring from the six years of my positive experience of my father. There is an image from a very early period: my father is sitting at the desk and I am on his lap, and we are watching a spider trying to climb up the round black smooth wood of the desk clock. The time seems infinitely long, and the spider keeps slipping back and trying once again, and it is always terrifying and lovely to see its long legs, which might suddenly also set off in our direction, and to have the security of my father's lap: nothing can happen to me. And it is exciting to see the world like that. I have never been afraid of spiders – unlike many of my contemporaries. Perhaps that is because of this earliest experience.

Another image: my father is sitting in his chair and I am on his lap. He is smoking his Sunday cigar and blowing great smoke rings for me in the air. I can put my index finger into them. It's an exciting game, even more fleeting and more beautiful than blowing soap bubbles.

And a third image: on Sunday mornings we used to lie in our parents' beds and play 'fighting'. I, the younger one, lay with my father, and we would fight against my big sister. I felt the nearness, warmth and strength of my father – that was my advantage, no matter who 'won', and that made up for the everyday superiority of my sister. The lines from Paul Gerhardt's hymn,

> When need and tribulation strike
> to sit in his lap,

and Paul Gerhardt's poetry with its imagery of God the mother, the mysticism and nearness of God to human beings – that was the religious parallel to this experience, and it has never completely left me even in pain and lostness.

Alongside these primal experiences I also have primal images, and these are embodied by the second important man in my family: my grandfather, an old-fashioned pastor in a village in Brandenburg; he more closely resembled the *image* of God. With white hair and a white beard, he seemed to me to be a gracious patriarch until in old age my mother told me of his sometimes rigid treatment of his children, which for me produced some blemishes in the ideal image of him that was cherished in the family and the community. On Sundays there was a holy stir around him: his wife, the housemaid and two spinster daughters looked after him. There was an egg for breakfast, but only for him; the rest had the usual fare: bread with plum jam. Then he preached in the whitewashed church with the sky-blue wooden ceiling. Between the first sermon and the second sermon in the next village he got another egg, this time in a kind of non-alcoholic egg-nog. But coachman Herrmann was already standing outside with horse and carriage – in good weather often an open landau, in bad weather a closed black coach – to go to the next church. At noon we met him on the high road and were allowed to get into the carriage for the ride back. The tension was over. The Sunday roast was waiting. The third village, where he sometimes had to give an afternoon sermon, did not have a church; in any case the people were not thought of as churchgoers and it wasn't so important.

Some days ago I found a very ragged picture book, *In the Heavenly Land*, which this grandfather had given to me, 'Our little darling', as the dedication read. I was two and a half years old when I got it. I had kept it for my children because I thought it quite charming, and I must have read it avidly, given its battered state, even though the pages were of thick glossy paper. In this heavenly book I now rediscovered with terrifying clarity my early Christian socialization and my early picture of God.

> In heaven above there live
> many dear little angels.
> They have white robes
> and little golden wings.
> They are so sweet and charming,
> so pious and wonderfully nice.
> They tell one another stories
> and sing as loudly as they can.

These little angels are obviously female; they sweep the blue room of heaven, clean, wipe, weed the garden and make things for Christmas with a blonde-haired feminine Christ child who has a starry robe. God the Father up there in the starry sky and St Nicholas are the only male figures. With his long white beard and hair and the host of female angels around him, with his graciousness and affection for the smallest angel child, this God the Father seemed to me to be my grandfather writ large. There was no problem with a male Trinity here: God's Son had become a feminine Christ child and the heavenly hosts had become gender-specific feminized angels, working in accordance with their role. (Women nowadays may be making God's Son Jesa Christa, but the 'Popular Art and Popular Education Publishing

Company', the publishers of *In the Heavenly Land*, got there first!). Anyway, God the Father – like my own grandfather – stood out among this bustling host of women: gracious, spiritual and exalted.

Gracious, spiritual and exalted – that was something, and in the family of women in which I grew up, I played this off against feminine petty-mindedness. My Father God, who constantly seemed to be standing at my side, was also gracious, spiritual and exalted. I prayed to him for things. My mother thought this blasphemous. I prayed to be allowed to wear knee stockings instead of scratchy long stockings as soon as it thawed. A symbol of freedom! I didn't want to be a boy – the lifestyle of the Hitler Youth of my time was not attractive – but I wanted to have their freedom. Rationality, sovereignty, wit and worldliness seemed to me to have free rein among men, teachers, remote uncles. Here I felt a lack in myself and other women. Here I sought identity. In my search for otherness, masculine interests, the Father God was on my side. I took the presence of my mother for granted, like air to breathe and daily bread. But her anxiety and worry, in which I could no longer identify with her, have been a lifelong problem for both of us.

However, I didn't know precisely in what direction I wanted to break out. 'Let me become a man', as some girls used to sing at the time, was not my dream. I wanted to get away from women's circles. I liked a few women who had poise, grace, stature and a mind. All other options were open. I hardly longed at all for a 'right' father. The images of the Prussian father which were instilled in us right from our infant school in Potsdam, like the soldier king who snatches the flute away from his son and has the cat he is fond of shot before his eyes; who beats up his soldiers, shouting, 'You *shall* love me', were grotesque ones of which I had no experience, and they nipped in the bud any longing I might have had for specific fathers. The Christian interpretation of this Prussian father in Jochen Klepper's book *The Father*, with his abysmally deep conflicts between faith and obedience, was always very remote from me personally. Here sado-masochistic images of Father and God emerged which women later thought that they rediscovered among theologians.

At the same time, here probably many of their own anxieties and personal experiences were catapulted on to theology.

But I certainly did once have a longing for a father. A schoolfriend who was giving extra tuition was criticized for the quality of her teaching. Suddenly her father was there on her side: 'My daughter always gives of her best!' I would have loved to have had such a father who was always unconditionally on my side.

Last night I asked a friend, a practising Catholic, what God the Father means for her. 'Nothing,' she said. 'My own father did so little to back me up, to boost my self-confidence – indeed he thoroughly destroyed it – that I prefer to imagine God as Spirit, Holy Spirit. That's the freedom that I need.'

Another friend, a liberal Protestant, suddenly discovered her identity in the loving arms of the Goddess. Parallel to that it is becoming increasingly clear to her how much her father, a loving patriarch, has robbed her of any sense of being valued. And I can see how no patriarchal father has distorted my own picture of God the Father.

In recent years God the Father has been put in the dock, has been accused and mocked. But behind all the sometimes absurd charges, including that of having torn Christian religion apart, there is a piece of personal history which those who have had other experiences must treat seriously. Once again the risk should be taken of detaching personal history from Christian history, in order to embark on the justified concern of a criticism of religion.

With my 'positive' relationship to the Father God I sometimes felt quite alone, for those who had become sensitive to the intertwining of their own experiences and the biblical images were at first rare. Now I know that the image of God the Father was also important for many other women in their socialization. For the *Concilium* issue on God as Father, Irene von Bourbon Parma wrote that she prayed in the Lord's Prayer to a God, 'with whom I look for protection, although I know that he wants me, as a human being, to go my own way – in faith'.

But independence and freedom have become complicated ways for women nowadays. These problems came home to me first when my feminine existence with children, housekeeping and professional work filled every moment, and this existence was like the cleaning, sweeping, singing angels in heaven. The view of the world that I wanted to abandon had got hold of me again. The pastor in it was now my own husband; not a pastor in the old fashioned style but a pastor without many demands. Only – the helping hosts, the clan of women, were now condensed into my own person. The dreams of God and freedom had to be internalized or projected on to the beyond. Inwardly there were protected zones. But here the soul was separated from the body. There were hopes for the future. Yet in the end these were old Christian emergency solutions which I didn't want. Where could freedom become physical, and eternity become present again? How could that be reconciled with belief in the Father?

At that time images of goddesses were cropping up in women's groups, goddesses who hold the universe in their embrace, images of alternative existence and alternative culture, the earth, nature and the interconnection of all things. After a visit to Egypt I liked above all the images of Knut embracing the universe with extra-long arms. This was an image which matched my life and which I absorbed into myself. That was the pattern and fabric of life which came to me: the 'petty-mindedness' in which women often (have to) live changed into a network of relationships from which life comes. But – where did that leave God the Father? I didn't experience any great personal conflicts like many other women around me. I didn't see any Either-Or. Was it naivety? Or was it perhaps that my Father God was big and generous enough, so that all other possible images could be coped with? The one who had for so long given and promised me independence and freedom was now – or so it seemed to me – standing there laughing and seemed to say, 'Do what you like. What you are doing is right. With me there is room for everything which arises out of pleasure, out of the deepest human needs. "In my Father's house there are many mansions." ' Were my experiences and images of my father behind this?

The New Testament, which we began to read again, confirmed this view: Jesus himself addressed his Father as Abba, that tender, intimate word full of nearness, warmth, everydayness and confidence, almost a slang word which children used on the streets. And to those who followed him and had left everything, fathers and mothers, house, brothers, sisters, children, lands, he promised that they would find it all again. But – no fathers, only brothers; no 'house', but 'houses' (Mark 10.29f.). The early community was a community without patriarchal structures and it was a pluralist community, without those later principles of faith which are around even today: unity goes before truth. The Our Father arises out of the spirit in which discipleship comes about as a result of pleasure and passion and not on the basis of self-denial; not on the basis of breaking the will, but in accord with the will of God who wills our will: 'Be it to you as you will' (Matt.15). Church talk is often miles away from such thought. Nowadays, when the word 'father' takes on too many patriarchal connotations for me, I try to replace father with mother, and in so doing can feel the image of parents being extended and enriched. However, the image of God the Father always becomes destructive for me when God is entrenched dogmatically as Father. There love of the Father God dies even for me.

However, much that is traditionally associated with the image of God the Father has become questionable for me, and I am trying to see it critically and perhaps also afresh. There is the image of the Father who gives up his Son and wants his sacrifice. It is increasingly difficult for many people to follow this theory of sacrifice which is also present in hymns, in the liturgy, in the Lord's Supper and the eucharist. And when Paul speaks of the Father 'giving up' the Son I cannot follow him; I cannot take over his speculations about the participation of God in the death of Jesus as thoughts on which I can reflect. I see God as the Father of Jesus who witnesses the death of his child with as much bewilderment and pain as any earthly father. The earth quaked, the curtain in the Temple was rent – so the Bible tells us: these were signs of the pain of God whose creation, the earth, is part of himself. The earth, his body, expresses pain.

A second critical thought followed from that. I think that the earth is part of God. We have forgotten this knowledge of the presence of God, of his holiness and presence in creation, in the name of a Father God who for most people expresses transcendence and exaltation. I can see from the functions of parents the one-sidedness in which we have landed ourselves. If we understand God in terms of parental images, then the father's function is that of procreation. That God the Father begets is familiar to us, and we also find it in the Bible. However, procreation is a relatively impersonal function. Just as the father who begets a child can remain extremely impersonal and loosely attached to it, so in the name of the Father God we have got used to seeing God and creation as two separate entities side by side. In order to make a new connection and bind God to his creation, we must part company with solitary father-images and also use mother-images of giving birth here. Only then will it again become clear to us that this earth which comes from God is a piece of God and so belongs to God – not as a possession but more as part of himself – and that any damage to it and exploitation of it affects God himself. Here I see my pattern and fabric of life, see it confirmed and acknowledged. The kind of transcendent father-image without a mother-image which has arisen in our culture has obscured our view of the immanence of God and has cheated Christianity and all of us of the centre of the Christian religion: the incarnation and indwelling of God in creation. Here we must extend our images of God and fill them with old/new life.

The new generation of fathers which can be seen now and again can help us to experience fathers anew, and associate them no longer with transcendence, distance and omnipotence but with corporeality, nearness to the earth and working relationships. So I can imagine a creative change in the problems caused by the image of the father for our Christianity. I myself believe in God the Father and hope for new fathers.

God as Mother

Jürgen Moltmann

I used to pray to God the Father, not to God the Mother. To address God as Father is a universal practice, known throughout Christianity. I first came across talk of 'God – our Father and our Mother' in an address by Pope John Paul I. His pontificate was only brief. The introduction of this way of speaking may be the only thing that he is remembered for. I then kept hearing talk of God the Mother from feminist theologians and also tried occasionally to use it in prayer myself. A theoretical intention to supplement the male father-image in the Godhead with a female mother-image is one thing; what we do in prayer is another. In prayer one feels what 'works' and what does not 'work' in a personal relationship to God. The forms of address used in prayer are a touchstone for all theology. We are quite familiar with God being thought of and addressed as 'Mother' from non-Christian and pre-Christian religions. The great mother of the world, Mother Earth, the mother of all living beings – the names of the goddesses of life and death are numerous, as is the religious experience which is expressed by them. In India the Goddess is Kali, the dark goddess, after whom Calcutta was named. In the present-day introduction of talk of God as Mother, it is obvious that ways divide: some look for the pre- or post-Christian 'Goddess' and abandon Christianity, while others want to extend a one-sided male Christianity with a paternalist stamp through a motherly women's Christianity.

One might suppose that Christianity is a religion of the Father. However, historically speaking that is not the case. It only took on this form as a result of its connection with Roman patriarchalism, the religion of Jupiter and the rights of the father. The religion of the Father is older than the original Christian faith and has different motives. God is very rarely addressed as 'Mother' in the history of Christianity. Where maternal images are used for God's care and protection, they tend to be metaphors rather than forms of address. It was some of the representatives of more recent feminist theology who first called for possibilities for women to identify with the Godhead, in order to experience God as Mother. In worship in the United States the 'Our Father' is sometimes replaced by a prayer to 'Our Father and our Mother in heaven' or to 'Our Parents in heaven'. However, that seems to me to be artificial and not spontaneous.

This 'message' reached me personally only at the beginning of the 1970s, in a spiritual, theological and cultural situation which I can describe quite precisely. The great challenge at the end of the 1960s and beginning of the 1970s was Marxism. With Fidel Castro's Cuban revolution and Che Guevara, the liberation of the oppressed and exploited masses began, and not just in Latin America. The Czech 'Socialism with a human face' of Alexander Dubcek promised the liberation of people in the 'Second World'. The Neo-Marxism of the 'critical theology' of Horkheimer and Adorno promised a 'new thought'. In the course of these movements the religious criticism of Feuerbach, Marx and Freud became the 'beginning of all criticism' (Marx) of the economy, society and the state, and therefore also the beginning of all criticism of the church and theology. The criticism became compulsory reading for every theologian and an obvious examination subject. The critique of religion also became the starting point for the new critical theology which we called 'political theology'. Some of us attempted to root the Marxist critique of religion in the criticism of religion by the Old Testament prophets and to go beyond it in that way. I myself developed a theology of the cross which was a decided criticism of religion (in *The Crucified God. The Cross of Christ as the Foundation and Criticism of Christian Theology*, 1972, English Translation, London and New York 1974). All religious projections end on the secular cross of Christ – grief is the experience of God: the choice is between the crucified Christ and the gods of power and capital. At that time we took up the religious critique of Feuerbach, Marx and Freud, and made it more radical, in order to arrive at a new theology. Anyone who had not gone through the critical 'fiery stream' (which is what the German 'Feuerbach' means) was regarded as naive and unsound for not being able to distinguish between his own fantasies and the wholly other reality of God. 'God the Father', regarded as a projection of the father of the family, of the father of the people, or even of the 'Pope', on to an imaginary heaven, had already been consumed in the fire of this criticism of religion. That was not just an 'opium of the people' (Marx) but simply an 'opium for the people' (Lenin) in a religious guise. According to the prophetic understanding the God of Israel is not Zeus the 'Father of all', nor even the 'Father of the fathers of the land', or whatever deity paltry potentates on earth might appeal to for a heavenly gift of divine grace.

For Christians, God is solely and exclusively the 'Father of Jesus Christ', Jesus' divine mystery which he called 'Abba'. Only those who see in Jesus the brother of men and women, only those who see Jesus as the humiliated Son of Man on the cross, 'see the Father'. The rest is the Ninth Symphony and religious fantasy. In view of the senseless suffering of creatures on the earth there is no natural reason for calling God 'Father'. Only the Christ who endures all this suffering makes this address to God possible and meaningful. I believe that when I prayed the 'Our Father', I never thought of my physical father, but always only of Jesus and his 'Abba' prayer, and I attempted to include my father with his experiences of suffering in this prayer in a brotherly way, as he himself certainly also did with me. In my theological education, for my generation Karl Barth's strictly christocentric view of the Our Father God was a liberation from religious illusion and suspect religion.

I am telling all this in such detail to explain why initially the phrase 'God the Mother' neither excited me nor offended me. The justifications for it seemed to me to be so naively religious that they immediately collapsed in the face of Feuerbach's criticism: if men call God 'Father' in order to be able to find an identity and now women call God 'Mother' in order to discover themselves in religious terms, what would donkeys call God? Is the Godhead just a screen for all possible projections, with the slogan 'What's your fancy?' Is Christian faith a religious supermarket? From a historical perspective, some historical feminists – I am thinking of the 'Goddess' movement, not those who adopted approaches along the lines of liberation theology and social psychology – rode in on the religious wave which was started in connection with the oil crisis in 1973. Wasn't this wave used to drive the critical and revolutionary spirit out of church and society? Without being refuted, all criticism of religion was pushed on one side, and 'religion' was again tolerated because 'the religious' was somehow said to be constructive. Jung was read again, instead of Freud, and he was promoted to become the religious father of post-Christian feminism, satisfying the wishes of many women for gentle archetypes. It may be that the criticism of religion by the prophets, the Marxists and critical theologians is 'typically masculine', but as long as God as 'Mother' is required only on grounds of appropriate feminine representation, as it were to fulfil a quota in heaven, and no account is taken any longer of rational criticism of religion, this naivety seems to me to be questionable. Of course the issue would need to be discussed at greater length. If 'Christian history' is uncoupled from family history, as Elisabeth Moltmann-Wendel suggests, then it also frees men and women from family pressures, as happened in the stories of Jesus' disciples. The mythical primal forces of fathers and mothers lose their power in those who set out with Jesus for the messianic future.

Where, then, are feminists still coming to grips with Feuerbach, Marx and Freud?

It was only in connection with my work on a 'social doctrine of the Trinity' that I discovered for myself the significance of the femininity of the *ruach*, the Holy Spirit. A pupil brought me the first sermon given by Count Zinzendorf in Pennsylvania, in which in 1741 he had proclaimed the 'motherhood of the Holy Spirit' for his 'community of brothers and sisters'. The historical roots of this statement were soon explained. Zinzendorf had come upon it through the homilies of Macarius which had just been republished. The Syrian church fathers were fond of addressing *ruho* – the Holy Spirit (feminine) – as 'divine mother'. They gave two reasons for this: the 'Spirit' promised in the Gospel of John is the 'paraclete': 'He will comfort you as one whom his mother comforts' (John 15.26; Isa.66.13). The believers are those who are 'reborn' from the Spirit of God (John 3.5), and so the Spirit is the 'mother of believers'. According to the gnostic Gospel of Thomas Jesus himself called the Spirit his 'Mother'. On Ethiopian icons the Trinity is occasionally depicted as a divine family: God the father, the Spirit the mother, Jesus the child. Augustine still wrote polemic against that, which shows how widespread the notion was. It contains important correctives to the other trinitarian conception of God the Father with the 'two hands', Son and Spirit (to be found in Irenaeus), since it presents the indescribable divine mystery as a community of being, as the inward community of love which is matched on earth by the relationship of love, the fellowship of the community, the solidarity of society and the sympathy of all creatures.

Whereas the conception of God the Father is bound up with the creation and the distance of the Creator from his creatures, the maternal mystery of the Holy Spirit contains the more intimate relationships of outpouring, indwelling and mutual influence. 'Grace and the gifts of grace', the 'Spirit and the powers of the Spirit', form community and permeate creatures without alienating them or destroying them. What tradition has described as the innermost power of the trinitarian mystery, the 'perichoresis', i.e. the reciprocal surrender and interpenetration of persons, is experienced by human beings in the Spirit: 'He who abides in love abides in God and God in him' (I John 4.16). Reciprocity is the principle of trinitarian community. Reciprocity is also the principle of the mystical experience of God. Finally, reciprocity is the principle of any community of women and men worthy of the name human, in mutual respect and reciprocal devotion. The social doctrine of the Trinity says that only this reciprocity, that is, the community but not the peculiarites of the individual persons of God, is capable of being portrayed. As John 17.21 says: 'That they may all be one, even as you, Father, are in me and I in you, that they may be one in us!' The trinitarian community is not reflected in human relationships either in the Fatherhood of the Father or in the Motherhood of the Spirit, but only in community with the human Son. In true human community men and women have 'all things in common' (Acts 4.32) except their personal identity. This community is the end of patriarchalism and is not a new version of matriarchy, but a messianic community of women and men, parents and children, without privileges and without disparagement.

The mystery of the Spirit has particularly fascinated me within the framework of this social doctrine of the Trinity. I have introduced trinitarian prayers into my services in the Stiftskirche in Tübingen, as has my colleague Eberhard Jüngel, and I have been particularly concerned about prayer in the Spirit to the Spirit. I have not only prayed 'Come, Holy Spirit' but also invoked 'the mother of all that lives', the 'spirit of life' and 'the power of rebirth', and have attempted to express the sighing of the Spirit in tormented creation. Hildegard of Bingen has helped me most to understand the breadth, beauty and intimacy of the Spirit:

> The Holy Spirit is lifegiving life,
> Mover of all and root of all created being,
> he purifies the universe from uncleanness,
> he blots out guilt and anoints the wounds,
> so he is shining light, worthy of praise,
> raising and reviving the universe.

One need only change the gender in this hymn to discover God the Mother of all and the power of the rebirth of the cosmos. Then one recognizes, as Elisabeth Moltmann-Wendel says, that 'The earth is a part of God'. In this sense I believe in God 'the Mother' and pray to the Holy Spirit, 'the mother of all that lives', in whom we and all other creatures, 'live, move and have our being' (Acts 17.28).

4

'Who do you say that I am?'

Peter's confession and Martha's confession

A joint Bible study at the General Assembly of the
Reformed World Alliance, Seoul, 15-26 August 1989

I

Introduction

Elisabeth: Who do you say that I am?

This question arises nowadays for many Christian men and
women who previously were silent and are now reflecting on who
Christ is for them: a black, a yellow, a liberating, a comforting
Christ. They want to find an answer to this for themselves and no
longer want just to be represented.

This question arises above all for women who in the two-
thousand-year-long history of the church have stood in the
shadow of their fathers and brothers and husbands, who have
become accustomed to keep quiet on theological questions, and
for whom patriarchs and church leaders have answered.

All over the world today, within their different social contexts,
from their various forms of life and everyday experiences, women
are looking for answers to what Christianity means for them.

Who do you say that I am?

So this morning we are going to try, from our different cultures
and churches, but above all from the different perspectives of the
sexes and their experience of life, to reflect on who Christ is for
us.

Jürgen: When God created human beings in the beginning, he
created them 'male and female' (Gen.1.27), and when his Spirit
comes on all flesh at the end, 'sons and daughters' will prophesy
(Joel.3.1).

The 'whole gospel for the whole world' can only be seen with female and male eyes, only be understood with male and female hearts, and only be borne witness to by a new community of women and men. For too long we have heard only half the gospel, with the male half of humankind. It is important today to understand it completely in the fullness of the female and male creation of humankind and with the fullness of the Spirit that comes upon sons and daughters. It therefore goes without saying that men and women confess their faith together and interpret the gospel together. If the truth is to be attested credibly, it must be confessed by the mouth of 'two witnesses'. That is an old rule. When Jesus sent out his disciples for the first time, he sent them out into the villages and towns of Israel 'two by two' (Luke 10.1). Nowadays that should mean that women and men confess their faith together.

Elisabeth: We are going to listen to one another. We are not going to be anxious about differences, but concerned for our different histories. We are not going to play off the eloquence of the one against the other's still unpractised way of talking. We are going to become interested in and curious about what is alien to us. And we should not immediately seek unity, but first investigate the wealth and variety of our faith. In so doing we are going to look at the Bible afresh, and see what it looks like from the perspectives of women and men.

But first of all we are going to ask each other: Who are you? We are going to get to know one another, where we come from, how we live, and how we feel this morning in this great gathering. We are going to break down some of the strangeness and get a bit closer together.

My suggestion is that in every group *women* should begin to introduce themselves.

II

The mystery of Christ

Jürgen: The biblical text from which the question 'Who do you say that I am?' comes is in the Gospel of Mark, 8.27-35.

1. Our story is about the question 'Who is Jesus?', on different levels: in popular opinion, according to the disciple Peter, and according to Jesus himself. In the Gospel of Mark it stands right between the miraculous healings of the sick and the no less amazing parables of Jesus about the kingdom of God, which precede it, and his way to Jerusalem, his condemnation and his death on the cross on Golgotha, which follow. Previously Jesus was the wonderworker to whom the suffering people brought their sick. From this moment on he becomes the man of grief, who shares the people's suffering to the point of torture and murder. Previously he has acted, subsequently he is acted on. This is in fact a turning point in his life: Jesus suddenly comes up against this question about himself.

Was it a straight question, or did he just want to make his disciples think? Was it his own question, or was it just a multiple-choice question? Because we suppose that we know so much about Jesus, and know so many of his titles from the history of the church, we often think that Jesus himself would surely have known who he was and must have been sure of himself. But according to the description in the Gospels, that was evidently not the case. The earthly Jesus does not know himself. He is a mystery to himself. He first learned to know himself under the guidance of the Spirit of God and to the echo of human faith. As the Gospels describe things, he lived in remarkable openness to his future. Of course these Gospels present his life story in the light of his end on the cross, and his presence in the Spirit by virtue of his resurrection. Therefore they lay on his life that mystery which is called the 'messianic secret', and present Jesus in such a way that he himself remains a mystery until his revelation on the cross and in the resurrection. But they could not have said this of him had not the reminiscences of him confirmed it. So our starting point is that Jesus' question about his mystery is a straight one and not a riddle. Jesus is as dependent on the knowledge and confession of men and women as on the faith of men and women in healing the sick. He is dependent on knowing himself with the eyes of the people, his disciples, male and female, and with the eyes of the God whom he called 'Abba' in such a childlike way. He also needs our knowledge today, since from the beginning there has been this inner reciprocity between Jesus and faith, between the Spirit of God and the child of God, from which the healing of this sick world comes. Certainly our faith is an echo of the sound which proceeds from Jesus. But echo and answer are part of any good music, especially when the concert is not yet at an end and we do not yet know the end. So it is extremely significant for Jesus and for the cause of Jesus when we say that he is. We ourselves are part of his history with this world, are fellow players, not onlookers. What answer do we give Jesus? How do we take part in his healing of this sick world?

2. Usually we answer like 'the people', literally 'men'. For the people who had heard the message of Jesus and seen his healing of the sick, Jesus is 'somewhat like' John the Baptist or Elijah or one of the prophets. After the murder of John the Baptist, Jesus came forward with the same message as the Baptist. Therefore recollection of John was still alive. According to Jewish expectation Elijah was to return before the end of the world. Anyone who proclaimed the nearness of the kingdom of God would inevitably be taken by some people as Elijah. To call Jesus one of the prophets gives him a high status, but robs him of his uniqueness. The people judge Jesus by analogies from their experience. We all do the same: when anything new surprises and disturbs us we look for something comparable from our experience. Agatha Christie has her Miss Marple solving the most puzzling crimes by 'recalling' old stories from her village of St Mary Mead.

Why is there what Ernst Troeltsch called this 'omnipotence of analogy' in our knowledge? Because any cognition is a re-cognition and because 'like can only be known by like', as Aristotle already remarked. When we hear of Jesus today we have no difficulty in forming a picture of him. Depending on our recollections, we call him a 'founder of a religion' like Buddha or a 'prophet' like Muhammed or a model of humanity like Confucius or a revolutionary like Che Guevara. We form a picture of him in accordance with our ideas, but the picture is less like him than like us. We confirm ourselves in him, not him in ourselves. As a result of such ideas we set up a wall between Jesus and ourselves and recognize almost nothing of him. If like is known only by like, then there is nothing new under the sun. If the law of analogy holds in knowledge, then we are incapable of perceiving anything else. We know only what confirms us. If like is known only by like, then we must say ironically that to the like, the like is a matter of 'indifference'. Only what is new and other is interesting. But we can perceive the other only when we are ready to change ourselves and our ideas. We can perceive something other only when we allow ourselves to be renewed. The question is not what our pictures make of Jesus but what Jesus makes of our pictures. That is the first reason why Jesus rejects what people say of him.

3. The disciples who had had close experience of him say more. Peter solemnly answers on their behalf, 'You are the Christ.' In so doing he takes up the central figure of Israel's hope: the Messiah king will liberate Israel and bring it home. The Messiah king will bring law and justice to all peoples from Zion. The Messiah king will bring humanity peace with nature. Through the Messiah king, God's kingdom comes into our ruined world and will make all things new. Just as Israel itself is God's 'firstborn son' among the peoples, so the Messiah king is 'God's Son' and all men are brothers. 'Son of the living God', the addition made by Matthew, mentions only the aspect of the Messiah king who will redeem the world which is related to God.

Jesus does not reject this title, but asks for it to be kept secret: the disciples are not to use it of him now. Why not? The following clash with Peter makes that clear: Jesus gives his own answer to the question about himself not by another picture or by a yet better title but by the prediction of a history which he will experience. He calls himself unemphatically 'Son of Man' and announces suffering, rejection and death which the Son of Man will experience. This is not the victory procession of the Messiah king hoped for by Israel, but the way of suffering trodden by the servant of God.

With his confession of Christ Peter wanted to be on the winning side, so he 'threatens' Jesus and seeks to talk him out of the way of suffering. The rock on which, according to Matthew, Jesus will build his church proves to be sand, on which one cannot build a house. The so-called prince of the apostles even becomes Satan for Jesus, i.e. he again confronts Jesus with the temptations which he had overcome in the wilderness before his mission. So Jesus drives him away: 'You do not think the thoughts of God but those of men' (Mark 8.31).

What wishes are hidden in our confession of Christ? 'With

Jesus you are always on the winning team', said a YMCA slogan in the USA. Christianity is the religion of the successful Western world. That attracts many people in Asia. Christianity is the face of freedom and leads people to ever greater progress, we are told in Europe. Since the emperor Constantine 'conquered' in the sign of the cross, must not our salvation history be a history of missionary success and cultural superiority? The church triumphant can be seen not only in Rome but also in Geneva and in Seoul.

'You are Christ.' Among us is that a confession of God or a confession of Satan, or is it always both, with motives which cannot be disentangled and a purpose which is ambiguous?

What does Jesus himself say that he is? We cannot be given certainty in faith by what our title Christ makes of Jesus, but only by what Jesus makes of this title.

We turn back once again and ask, 'Who do you say that I am?' What count are not the wishes of Peter but the experiences of Jesus. Jesus fills Peter's conception with his own history. Who do you say that I am? He does not yet know. His own life story and suffering will be the answer.

This confession of Peter's should really make us uncertain. Can we say anything at all? Can we give an answer? Can we say at all who Christ is?

III

Martha's Confession

Elisabeth: Who do you say that I am? In our story Jesus puts this question to his disciples, and Peter answers on behalf of the others, 'You are Christ, the Son of God' or 'the Son of the living God.'

'Where were the women, then?', ask many women, many Christian women throughout the world. Were they counted among the disciples, and did Peter answer for them?

Were they a small group who were part of the Jesus movement but were primarily responsible for looking after Jesus' disciples and giving them financial support? In that case surely so momentous a question would not have been put to them? They would probably have had no voice and no right to express their opinion. In our first community the local community preacher told me that as a woman I only had the right to *ask*, not to make any theologically binding statements.

We now know that not only men, but also women followed Jesus. Jesus had female as well as male disciples. It was a woman who showed him the way to suffering and death and anointed him king and prophet. It was a woman who made him saviour of the Gentiles, and she is now regarded as the apostolic forebear of all Gentile Christians. It was a woman who was first to hear the message of the resurrection and given the task of handing on this message. What would have happened had women in fact kept silent in the church? There would be no church.

Moreover we know that there were not only twelve male apostles but also female apostles, and that the early church attempted to be a community of women and men far removed from all patriarchal structures. But the history of Christianity has covered itself with a patriarchal crust and hidden the beginnings from us.

We can no longer infer from our story whether women were present, whether Peter spoke for them or whether the writer of the story thought that women were created for other activities. But we know another story from the Gospels where a woman confesses Jesus Christ, and I would like to set it alongside our first story; it is Martha's confession (John 11), and we find it in the story of the raising of Lazarus: 'You are the Christ, the Son of God, the one who is coming into the world.' Hitherto it has hardly found much recognition in Christianity, just as women too have hardly found recognition.

Some years ago, however, the American New Testament scholar Raymond Brown worked out that this confession is very similar to the well-known confession of Peter and comes very close to it. But it is spoken by someone else, Martha. In the Johannine communities it probably had the significance that Peter's confession had in other communities. The intention was not to disparage Peter, but he was to be regarded as just one among many others. A brake was to be put on the predominance of the twelve apostles, which was already making itself felt, and other personalities in the Jesus movement were to be put on the same level as them. Accordingly, it was not the power of an official ministry but the manifold charismatic capacities which made up the life of the church. Whereas there were communities in which Peter was regarded as the one who had made the supreme confession of Christ, there were other communities, like the Johannine community, which associated such reminiscences with the figure of Martha. Through this research we get a new view of the multiplicity of the early churches and above all a view of the significance of women in the church, in leading the community and in theology! This is a view which takes us beyond official ministries and males and teaches us to see the women with new eyes.

Above all, though, we get a new view of a woman, Martha, whom our Christian tradition had made a good housewife, a tradition which goes back to the famous story of Mary and Martha with Jesus in their home. In this story Martha is the good, diligent housewife, seeing to the welfare of the guest. She asks her sister Mary to help her instead of listening to Jesus, only to be reprimanded by Jesus: 'Mary has chosen the good part, and that shall not be taken from her.' Martha, a tragic female figure in our churches, is the one who has to see to the necessities of life and does not even find recognition. In Europe, the homes run by the deaconess organizations were named after her. The other story about Martha was forgotten, the story of her active, tenacious, lively role in the raising of Lazarus. But above all people forgot her confession of Christ, which stands alongside the famous testimonies on an equal footing.

If we look at it closely, it is even a confession of Jesus which goes a little way beyond the famous confessions in the New Testament. It is a remarkable passage, which challenges us to listen once again to the women of the New Testament: 'I believe,' says Martha, 'that you are the Christ, the Son of God, the one who is coming into the world.'

Christ, the Son of God – those are the testimonies in the New Testament on which there is agreement. We find them in all the Gospels. We hear them from the lips of Peter and the other disciples. We find this testimony as the real substance of what the Gospels seek to communicate to us. The stories are written – as we are told in John – 'that you may believe that Jesus is the Christ, the Son of God.' But in Martha's confession there is an addition, 'the Christ, the Son of God, the one who is coming into the world'.

Does that mean anything, and if so, what? Has it anything to say to us that differs from the confessions with which we are familiar?

Who do you say, Martha, that I am?

First of all let us look again at the context, the story, in which this confession is made. In the village of Bethany there live two sisters and a brother, Martha, Mary and Lazarus, who are among the closest confidants and friends of Jesus. When Lazarus becomes seriously ill, the sisters send for Jesus to come and heal him. But Jesus keeps them waiting. Only when Lazarus is dead does Jesus come, and is met on the way to Bethany by the ever quick, active and bold Martha, with the almost reproachful statement, 'Lord, if you had been here, my brother would not have died!' Then she adds an almost crazy hope, 'But even now I know that whatever you ask from God, God will give you.' Jesus replies, 'Your brother will rise again.' And the quick Martha reacts just as quickly with a statement which seems as if it came from a catechism, 'I know that he will rise again in the resurrection at the last day.' However, Jesus' answer is that *he* himself is the resurrection and the life, and whoever believes in him will never die. Eternal life is already here. All hopes are already fulfilled in faith here. Does Martha believe that? She answers with her distinctive confession of Christ, 'I believe that you are the Christ, the Son of God, the one who is coming into the world.'

The situations of these two confessions are very different.

In the former, Jesus was the one involved, and he wanted information about himself and the relationship of his disciples to him.

Here a woman is the one involved. She has been made deeply uncertain, has been affected by the death of her brother. Her confession is neither abstract nor neutral. She does not see herself on the winning side. Her confession is born of deep sorrow and forsakenness, of a break with all previous relationships, of a separation from what provided her personal and perhaps also her economic security.

In the first confession, the disciples are brought down from the exalted heights of the community of God to the way of death and the cross, from the hope for successful life to the way of the cross and the failure of personal expectations.

Here Jesus promises the woman involved, who has received this deadly blow, the overwhelming comfort that he himself is life and resurrection. He promises her life, not suffering; resurrection, not death; fulfilment here, not hope for the beyond.

In the first episode, the disciples answer that the one with whom they are experiencing the dawn of a new age is the Son of God. Here the woman answers with the same confession of Christ. But she brings the Son of God, God himself, firmly down into this world: 'You are the Christ, the Son of God, the one who is coming into the world.' For her Christ takes on colour, form, earthliness. The Christ becomes quite concrete and corporeal.

'The one who is coming into the world . . .' What is there special about this statement? The famous theologian Rudolf Bultmann helped me to understand this addition of Martha's. Bultmann says that this title, 'the one who is coming into the world', is the 'most significant' title alongside the other two, 'Christ' and 'Son of God', because it expresses most clearly 'the incursion of the beyond into the this-worldly'. The title is absent from all the other confessions in John, nor can it even be found in this connection elsewhere in the New Testament.

Now 'the one who is coming into the world' is a statement which Jesus often makes about himself in the Gospel of John. He is the light that has come into the world: 'I have come as light into the world, that whoever believes in me may not remain in darkness' (12.46). 'For this I was born, and for this I have come into the world, to bear witness to the truth' (18.37). 'I came from the Father and have come into the world' (16.28). The world, the cosmos, has a double meaning here: it is the object of God's love and the recipient of his revelation, and at the same time it is the power which rebels against God and is rejected. 'He came to his own and his own received him not.'

The woman takes up Jesus' testimony to himself and in so doing achieves an immediate nearness to him that no other witness to Christ has subsequently achieved. The contrasts which she addresses here could not be greater: on the one hand God – on the other hand the divided cosmos. God hands himself over. The light shines in darkness. God enters the world. Martha makes this statement when she has experienced Jesus as the one who is light in the darkness, who gives life in death and the pains of death: warmth, nearness, hope. She does not make this statement when everything is back to normal and her brother is alive again. She makes it when nothing but the presence of Jesus is the light in her own darkness. Nothing is thought of as exalted, other-worldly, victorious. No heavenly solution is envisaged. Martha mentions the conflicts which from a human perspective are irreconcilable: God and the world, the beyond and this world, the healing power and the power of death. But in her experience of the nearness of Jesus the incursion of the beyond into this world has already taken place. 'You are the Christ, the Son of God, the one who is coming into the world.'

We know Martha from the Bible as the sober, pragmatic one, as the one who gets down to things, in the kitchen and in life. 'He already stinks,' she says of the corpse of her brother which is four days old. So Martha can identify in a uniquely matter-of-fact way the paradox that God has become man, that the beyond has broken into this world, that the old is past.

Here is, as Raymond Brown has said, a woman to whom 'the miracle of Jesus as the resurrection and the life is manifested'. Is that by chance? I don't think so. Christ, the life, reveals himself to women who give, sustain and hand on life.

We have looked at two confessions, from two different situations. We are not to set them over against each other but to put them side by side. We are to take seriously those who made them, and to recognize in the difference the wealth of our tradition. But we are above all to take seriously the suppressed tradition, situation, experience of women, and react to it.

Martha was forgotten and banished to the kitchen. Hardly anyone knows John's story and her confession. Peter makes history, church history, and is even known to any atheist. If the church is a community of women and men, then it should be understood not only 'in the Spirit' or eschatologically, but in concrete terms. That means learning to listen to the voices of the women, old and new.

Group discussions:
What do you know of the women of the New Testament?
What role do women play in your church?

IV

Confessing Christ and following Jesus

Jürgen: Jesus' own answer to the question of the Christ is not a theoretical answer but a practical one. We find it on the way of his passion. So he responds to the 'messianic secret' with the announcement of his suffering. Anyone from now on who wants to know who Jesus truly is must *go* with him, and on the *way* he will learn who Jesus truly is. 'No one can truly know Christ unless he follows him in his life,' said the radical Anabaptist Hans Denk at the time of the Reformation. That is not a moral law; what is meant is that we know Jesus rightly when we live with him. In living communion with Jesus we learn to understand him, not only with our head but also with our heart, not only with head and heart but with all our experiences in the joys and pains of life. We recognize and we believe, we feel and taste, his communion in our life. That can be called *total knowledge of Christ*. Christology and christopraxis become one. Confessing Christ and following Jesus coincide. They are not fused just when we suffer for the faith, but already when we begin to live in faith. In those experiences which we have in the community of Christ, the fantasies which we have of Jesus and which we express in the title Christ fall apart. We experience him as the brother who goes with us and takes us with him on the way of life.

2. Let's look again at the Gospel of Mark. There Jesus forbids his disciples to use the title Christ, which Peter has just offered him, but he teaches publicly that the Son of Man must suffer many things, that he will die and rise again to eternal life. He turns not only to his disciples, men and women, but also to the poor people – *ochlos* in Greek, *minyung* in Korean – and asks for volunteers to follow him:

'If anyone will follow me . . .'

Who is this 'Son of Man' with whom Jesus identifies himself?

Why must this 'Son of Man' suffer much in this world, as we are told here? I think that this 'Son of Man' (from Daniel 7) is not a private person but denotes a corporate person. It is the 'human person' as created in the image of God, the child of righteousness and peace. If this truly 'human person' comes into an inhuman world of violence and injustice, then he will have to 'suffer much', for he will experience the conflict of this world in himself. The 'Son of Man' has really already suffered, from the beginning of human history: he suffered when Cain murdered his brother Abel; he suffered when God's people Israel were oppressed and persecuted. The Son of Man suffers wherever people are humiliated, insulted, oppressed and exploited by others. Jesus takes upon himself this destiny of the Son of Man in an inhuman world. Therefore that suffering which we call the 'suffering of Christ' is not just limited to Jesus: according to Hebrews 11, the 'suffering of Israel' is also part of the 'shame of Christ'. And the sufferings of the poor and sick people – are they not also part of the 'suffering of Christ'? The image of the great judgment of the world in Matthew 25 tells us that the 'Son of Man' is present among us in 'the least of his brothers and sisters'. Jesus did not come into the world of victors. He went to the victims and himself became a victim to redeem the world. I understand this to mean that through the way of his passion Jesus brought the humanity of God into this inhuman world, the peace of God into our conflicts, the divine righteousness into our misery. He suffered injustice and violence, in order to redeem humankind from injustice and violence and to set up the human kingdom of the Son of Man among us.

3. Those who follow Jesus and try to stand up for human rights and human dignity in this world will also experience something of the suffering of Christ. They will 'be rejected', says Mark. Let's take an easier word: on the way of Jesus we will have to reckon with the *contempt* of other people. We all depend on the respect of others, for we always also see ourselves with the eyes of others. What happens in my country if we take a public stand on the peace question or the question of justice for the Third World? In my country, no one is persecuted and imprisoned, nor do people have to fear for their lives. But you are suddenly isolated by the silence of colleagues and neighbours. Malicious gossip is spread

behind your back. You are regarded as an 'idiot' or a 'traitor' to the interests of your own people. You find yourself on a secret police list as a 'dangerous person'. Then the telephone is tapped, the post opened and so on. In some cases it all begins with innocuous civic reprisals, and in other cases it ends with dangerous measures. As we know, what begins with lack of respect can end with extermination.

Do we get to know Jesus in such experiences? I think so, since for the sake of the humanity of God we are then taking part in that 'suffering of the Son of Man' and are sure of his nearness. I know that people have learned to pray and believe again through protesting against nuclear weapons by the barbed-wire fences of the munition depots. You can detect the presence of the living God very clearly when confronted by the inhuman means of mass destruction.

4. Jesus goes on to talk of 'denying oneself' and 'taking up the cross' after him. I personally have had hardly any experience of this, but we all share in the collective experiences of the community of Christ in its martyrs. The cross was the answer of the powers-that-be in Jerusalem to the message and the life of the human Jesus, which was lived in harmony with God. Execution was the answer of the authorities in Germany to the resistance against injustice in which Dietrich Bonhoeffer took part. Murder was the answer of the death squad in El Salvador to the way in which Archbishop Arnulfo Romero supported his people. It would not be good for us to suppress these dangerous memories. I think that martyrs, like Jesus himself, have become a seed of hope. For the end of the Son of Man is not death, but resurrection and life and the kingdom that will have no end. So we can regard his suffering as redemptive suffering, since it redeems our world from the shades of injustice and violence. And is not the suffering which men and women experience in his community also a liberating suffering?

V

'The one who is coming into the world . . .'

Elisabeth: 'You are the Christ, the Son of God, the one who is coming into the world.' What does that mean for us today? What has Martha's confession to say to us?

What does that mean, first of all, for women? What does it mean for those whose life, person and situation we have hardly noticed in the church, except in the necessary services which have kept the churches alive: serving, cooking, cleaning, helping, caring, holding honorary positions?

Who do you say that he is?

I would like to begin with Martha's own addition, 'the one who is coming into the world'. Which world is that? It is not the world of pulpits, bishops' thrones, church offices and conference tables. It is not the world of brothers-in-office, the brotherly church and the church authorities. It is not the world of gowns and the international uniform of male jackets.

It is the world where life is given, sustained and handed on. And that happens in clinics and kitchens, in conditions of poverty and in cramped hostels, in the struggle for the handful of rice, in lining up for food and in the daily fight against disorder and dirt. It is waged in dirty aprons, dressing gowns and jeans. It usually goes on invisibly and almost always is unpaid.

The world of women today is also the world in which physical violence, rape and incest are suffered far more than we suspect, where the powers of state and industry keep women in the lower-income groups, make them redundant more quickly than men, drive them on to the streets as prostitutes to earn their daily bread, making them goods which have to sell themselves. It is the world of silent humiliation, in which women are second-class citizens and helpers for men, with the result that many remain dependent all their lives and are treated like children. It is the world of solitude and isolation, in which many have to bring up their children by themselves, while the lifestyle of marriage and family is encouraged by society and expected by the churches. It is the world in which women nowadays are fighting all over the world and in very different ways for their views of life, for daily water and daily bread, and for self-determination and responsibility for themselves.

But it is also the world where women today are rising from death, contempt and non-being, are discovering their forces, using their heads, and demanding their human right to make this world a more humane place.

You are the Christ, the Son of God, the one who is coming into this world so that this world may not remain as it is.

Who is this Christ?

For many women nowadays he is no longer the victorious hero, at whose feet the peoples are to kneel, as missionaries have long proclaimed. Nor is he any longer the ruling king, to whom all is subject – as Western Christian ideology has long held. Nor is he any longer the Vatican male, from whom masculine Roman church government draws its legitimation.

For those women who have not been driven away by the masculinity of the church, the Christ is the human being whose humanity was so long hidden under his masculinity. He is a person who was happy, who groaned, who suffered grief, was tired and hungry, and could be offended. He is a person who was uncertain and made unsure of himself, as we are. He is a person who doubted in God and was never perfect, exalted, finished. He is a person who matured and grew. The most important thing that women have discovered is that he is a person who needed others and whose life's work is inconceivable without them. This Jesus was rubbed up the wrong way by other people; he was disappointed by other people; but he grew and matured to his life's work through other people. And it was above all women who stood by his side at the turning points of his life.

Today this Jesus who understood himself as someone in the pangs of creating a new world, who in his work and his life felt like a woman in labour, gives women courage to accept their womanhood and to keep on living for life, to continue the struggle for daily life, the life of children and old people.

What many Christian women think and say today is, 'I believe in the wholeness of the Redeemer.' Jesus was whole, fully human, and liberates us to be fully human like him. He liberates us to be women and men who are to live alongside one another equally and to share tasks in family, church and society.

And who is this God?

In the past history of the church and humankind women have endured life rather than shaped it, borne it passively rather than self-consciously moulded it. When women today come out of their kitchens and churches, when they seek to contribute their experiences in church and society, they need images of God by which they feel themselves to be strengthened. Our church and its language is full to the brim with male images of God: Lord, king, judge, ruler, creator. Nowadays we have rediscovered many of the forgotten feminine images of God in the Bible: God as mother, as a woman in the pains of childbirth, as nurse and midwife; God as the wife who has to cope with everyday chaos and while clearing it up comes upon the precious coin; God as the hen who takes her chickens under her wings; God as the mother eagle.

Women who give, sustain and hand on life need new life-giving, living images of God to guide them on their way. They need images of God to counter the world of force and destruction which they experience around themselves and among women. They do not need heroic images and fantasies of victory. 'God sits there weeping,' a woman wrote, 'because the beautiful carpet of creation which she wove with so much love has been destroyed, torn to pieces.' But just as in their own personal lives women have to go on, to keep on working, keep on hoping, so too they do not stop at the death of God but see God before them, wanting to weave a new pattern of life and inviting us to sit beside her and weave the carpet of the new creation with her.

That is the faith in the living God which Peter confessed; it is not exhausted in traditional images and names, but fills God's life with our life and our life with God's.

God is the living God whose child Jesus was human and who entered this world of violence, exploitation and isolation.

The beyond *has* broken into this world. With Martha we are called to believe in the resurrection and life *here* and to work and to weave towards it.

With Martha we are called to stop consoling ourselves with distant times. With Martha we are directed towards the tree of life, our only hope, in which all the crosses of this world begin to grow green again.

VI

Conclusion

'The one who is coming into the world . . .'

Jürgen: What does that mean for me? Who do I say that he is?

For me Jesus is the brother who has come into my world. When I was at the end of my tether and wanted to give up, he was there in the misery of my prisoner-of-war camp in 1945, and found me and led me on his way.

For me, Jesus became the bearer of a boundless hope which raises me up when I am cast down and gives me new courage when I fail.

In Jesus I have always detected something of the Spirit of the living God, of the Spirit which makes alive, the Spirit of resurrection.

Elisabeth: There are different ways, different cultures, different situations. There are two sexes, and we should take note of the variety of Christian faith.

But there is only one Christ, from whose life we all draw strength. We continue his life today by not making our own experiences absolute but by constantly making new space among us for his life, his story, his death and his resurrection. We make this room by listening to those who so far have had no room, and whose due is a place, a right and voice in our churches. So we say with our lives who he is: the Son of the *living* God, as Peter says, the Son of Man who constantly gives us new life in and through others.

5

The bent woman is made straight

A joint television service from the church in Sexau,
broadcast by ZDF on 15 October 1989

*Jesus was teaching in one of the synagogues on the sabbath.
And there was a woman who had had a spirit of infirmity for
eighteen years; she was bent over and could not fully straighten
herself. And when Jesus saw her, he called her and said to her,
'Woman, you are freed from your infirmity.' And he laid his
hands upon her, and immediately she was made straight, and
she praised God. But the ruler of the synagogue, indignant
because Jesus had healed on the sabbath, said to the people,
'There are six days on which work ought to be done; come on
those days and be healed, and not on the sabbath day.' Then
the Lord answered him, 'You hypocrites! Does not each of you
on the sabbath untie his ox or his ass from the manger and lead
it away to water it? And ought not this woman, a daughter of
Abraham whom Satan bound for eighteen years, to be loosed
from this bond on the sabbath day?' As he said this, all his
adversaries were put to shame, and all the people rejoiced at
all the glorious things that were done by him (Luke 13.10-17).*

Elisabeth: Any woman who hears this story of the woman who
was bent over could probably tell her own story about it: stories
of humiliations, injuries, stories of excessive burdens and illnesses
which prevented her from walking upright, which gave her
damaged vertebrae and later a hunched back. Let's look again
closely at this women's story.

It is a festival day, the sabbath, the Jewish Sunday. The service
is packed full, since everyone wants to see and hear Jesus, the
teacher and miraculous healer. He stands there, hemmed in by
the crowd. But his gaze goes out beyond all the great who have
pushed to the front and got themselves a good view. It goes out

beyond all the great men and all those who have big ideas about themselves and are self-important, and seizes on a woman. Not just any woman, but a woman whom all the other women tower above, who is so bent over that she can't even look up. He calls her over. I can imagine this scene vividly. All those with big ideas of themselves and good positions have to give way to this inconspicuous, bent figure. Now she stands centre stage, and all eyes are directed towards her. I can also imagine how embarrassing that is for her: she and her suffering are suddenly the focal point. In the same way, it is still unusual for many women in the church to see themselves, to take themselves and their problems seriously, and to voice their complaints.

God does not want women to be inconspicuous. God does not want women to remain invisible, to be humiliated and oppressed. He does not want them to bear burdens which finish them off. God does not want them to end up thinking of themselves as small, lowly, of little value. So Jesus brings the woman into the centre and draws attention to her, just as here in this service we want to draw attention to women.

And then this woman is told, 'Be free from your illness. Be free from what oppresses you and your body. Be free from what burdens you,

> from scorn,
> from contempt,
> from anxiety about the future.'

But that is easier said than done. How does she get a straight back again? How does she become whole? Healing does not just come about through words, nor will we too get rid of our oppression and repression by encouraging words alone. Jesus does more. He puts his hands on the woman, and in this stream of warmth, of concern and physical proximity, she can stand upright again. We touch one another when we are intimate. When we embrace again after being parted from someone – by a dispute or by physical separation – a stream of warmth goes through our bodies. That is what the woman must have experienced: all the muscles relax, and all the tensions are eased.

She had been sick for eighteen years: not just suffering but also socially segregated, isolated from other people. For according to the views of the time, anyone who touched her would similarly be afflicted by the evil spirit of the disease. Now someone is there who is not afraid of touching her; moreover, it is a man who breaks through the barriers to her, to her sex. All separations which isolate her as a sick person and, moreover, isolate her as a woman, are broken down.

Part of healing is that our loneliness is done away with. Part of healing is that someone breaks though the limitations that are laid on us by society.

Part of healing is that we experience attention, warmth and nearness. Part of the healing of women from all that oppresses and represses them is for us to be recognized as complete, whole persons: as persons with our own anxieties, cares, deformities, hopes and hidden capacities. In such a stream of warmth, women can stand upright. In such a warm stream of attention, concern and trust, we can stand upright.

For the woman, the world now suddenly looks different. Let's try to imagine for a moment what the world had looked like to this woman for eighteen years. Let's look down at the ground. It gets darker; we see the ground, the dust and what is just under our feet. And when we raise our heads and look up, we detect the difference: we see light. We see what is around us. We see what is above us. We get new perspectives, new views, new colours. The world looks different, wider, more complex. The change is overwhelming, and the woman thanks God.

But people immediately take offence at this action. The law decrees that nothing may be done on the sabbath, and such a healing may not take place. Those who dictate morality are furious at the breach of social and religious customs. And all for an inconspicuous, deformed woman! Jesus replies that the people who are giving vent to their fury here do not leave their cattle to perish on Sundays, but lead them to the water. They are concerned about the life of the cattle. He is concerned about the life of the woman. And then he calls her by a name which is unique in the Bible. He calls her a 'daughter of Abraham'. Previously people knew only 'sons of Abraham'. Now a woman, a sick woman who has just been healed, is put in the succession to Abraham, the father of faith. Not only do sons count for something in the community of Jesus; now daughters are given the same status.

They are not second-class, not the other sex, not simply married women. They have equal rights in the church of Jesus, and they too hand on the religious heritage. God does not just have strong sons. God also has daughters who are to be raised up and go through life with head held high. God does not want women just to bend their heads in church and say Yes and Amen, but to become visible as daughters of God, to use their heads, to contribute their perspectives and also to learn to say 'no'.

God calls women out of anonymity. God does not want any woman to remain inconspicuous. Jesus puts himself on the side of women and frees them from isolation. He helps the woman to live and to walk upright, and gives her equal rights in the community.

Jürgen: Any man who hears this story of Jesus and the woman who was bent over could probably also tell her story, but it would look rather different. Boys, too, are 'bent over', possibly from an early age, so that one day they become 'men', hard in taking and hard in giving. My own youth fell in the Third Reich and alternated between school and pre-military training: 'Whatever makes you hard is good for you', and, 'A boy does not cry'; if he is in pain he grits his teeth. 'Learn to control yourself, and then you will be able to control others and be a Leader.'

I can still hear these sayings which people used at that time to break us in and make us tough. They stripped away our sensitivity and feeling. We became afraid of ourselves and aggressive towards others: 'You're nothing; you can't do anything. You must make something of yourself, otherwise you'll always be an underdog.' That's how we were prepared for our struggle in life.

Who raises us up again? Who changes us back from being such men into people, whole people with a soul and body, understanding and feeling?

I recall the period after the war, when I returned from imprisonment broken and at odds with myself, having lost all my self-confidence. I had done nothing. I had only learned to make myself inconspicuous in order to get through: not to stand out, not to be punished. I was really bent over, mixed up and repressed. Self-confidence had turned into self-hatred and self-pity.

What raised me up? I believe that it was people who had

confidence in me, something that I did not believe possible. There was someone who loved me and in whose eyes I was good, whole and beautiful. My self-confidence grew in this miraculous experience. I regained self-respect, and my twisted soul slowly and increasingly came straight. I could tear apart the network of these youthful repressions. They no longer made any impression on me. I became a free person and risked walking upright with head high.

Why do I tell such a personal story, which is nobody's business? I have told it because I have also constantly seen similar experiences in others.

There is the handicapped student. He can only speak with a stutter. So no one listens to him. The other students think that he won't get anywhere anyway, and regard him as second-rate. When I got to know him, I had the impression that he could succeed, and to his surprise gave him a demanding topic for a major piece of work. He sailed through it, got a job and a wife, and finally has completely shaken off the paralysing feeling that he was handicapped by his handicap.

Then there is the shy student who never said anything in the seminar because she had no confidence, because the male students talked so loudly and for so long. When I noticed how clever she was, I said, 'You're leading the discussion in the next seminar.' Of course she didn't think that she could do it and would have loved to run away. But the discussion was splendid. She guided it in a quite marvellous way and many people were amazed at her. She went out with her head high. She had made the breakthrough. She had found a little piece of herself which had got lost in her anxiety.

Are there differences between the crippling pressures experienced by women and those experienced by men? It could be that at a very early stage men learn to pass on to others the buffeting that they themselves received. Masculine anxiety makes men aggressive; they then become very lonely. In the case of women it could be that they are patient, suffer, keep quiet and make themselves inconspicuous in order to preserve a relationship and not be lonely. They would rather lose their own self. But it is clear what a fatal effect both these attitudes have. One becomes a burden to the other: that is the law of a bent world, a world of deliberate violence and a tolerance which leads to disintegration, of men who stand upright and women who are bent over, of chattering women and silent men. Not a particularly human world!

A handicapped woman stood upright when Jesus healed her. She was crippled and bent over with pain.

We can live in the Spirit of Jesus and help one another to stand upright. Certainly we shall not become miraculous healers like Jesus. But we can bear the burdens together. Many of those who are handicapped say that the worst thing is not the physical handicap, but the social handicap which arises from the abhorrence of others. It is not the handicap that makes people ill but the fact that they no longer have confidence in themselves and begin to despise themselves. The social handicap of the handicapped is unnecessary. We can remove it, if in the spirit of Jesus we can affirm one another as we are. The mental grief of the handicapped is unnecessary. We can remove it, if we believe in the spirit of Jesus. Jesus believed in the woman who was bent over: in his eyes she was 'a daughter of Abraham', one of the elect, a kind of princess. So *he* healed her. But *she* stood *upright*. I believe that we, too, can do something of this kind in the spirit of Jesus: not show compassion which makes us dependent, but help people to help themselves. We always need just a little trust, a little sign of encouragement to put us straight and raise us up.

In the spirit of Jesus we sense the broad sphere of freedom in which every woman and every man can develop in his or her own way without arrogance, and also without anxiety. Let us open ourselves mutually to this space which God gives! Let us believe in one another!

6

The Theology of the Cross

The cross of Christ: the pain of the love of God

Jürgen Moltmann

At the centre of Christian faith stands a story: the story of the passion. That has to be taken quite literally, i.e. in the two senses of the word 'passion'. The story of Christ is the story of a great passion, a passionate hope. So, and precisely for that reason, at the same time it has also become the story of an unprecedented suffering, a deadly agony.

At the centre of Christian faith stands the passion of the passionate Christ. The passion story has this active and this passive side.

In former times people often overlooked the passion of Christ which led him to the passion. The man of sorrows then became the archetype of silent surrender to a wretched fate.

Nowadays, by contrast, people tend to overlook the passion, the suffering, which goes with any great passion. They would like to be blissfully happy and to suppress suffering. They anaesthetize grief and deprive themselves of feeling. Life without passion is impoverished. Life without readiness for a passion, for suffering, is paltry. Anxiety about suffering must be overcome just as much as fear of suffering. Otherwise hope cannot be reborn.

Let us pause at two stations on the story of Christ's passion and ask ourselves what happened there, in Gethsemane and on Golgotha.

1. Gethsemane

The passion story does not begin with the capture and torture of

Christ by the Roman soldiers. It begins much earlier. It really begins in the province of Galilee, at the moment when Christ decides to go with his disciples to Jerusalem, to the centre of power. His passion for the kingdom of God, the healing of the sick, the liberation of the downtrodden, the forgiveness of sins, would inevitably come up against its harshest enemies in Jerusalem, the priests of his people and the Roman occupying forces. His entry into Jerusalem was anything but triumphant: the people gathered and cried out, 'Blessed is the one who comes in the name of the Lord! Blessed is the coming kingdom of our ancestor David' (Mark 11.9-10). That makes it all the easier to understand the nervousness of those responsible for law and order, who were afraid of a popular rebellion. The man from Nazareth was getting dangerous. So he had to disappear, quickly and unobtrusively.

So far there is nothing special about this story. Many heroes, many freedom fighters, have gone to their deaths for their people with their eyes open.

In the case of Christ, however, there is something different, at first sight quite incomprehensible. In the night before the Romans arrested him, he went into the Garden of Gethsemane, took only three of his friends with him, and 'began to be distressed and agitated', as Mark puts it. Matthew says that 'he became sorrowful and anxious'. In other words, he was in despair. 'My soul is troubled to death,' he said, and asked his friends to watch with him.

At an earlier stage, too, Christ had often withdrawn at night in order to be alone with God in prayer. Here for the first time he did not want to be alone with God. He sought protection among his friends. Protection from whom? And then comes the prayer which sounds like a request: 'Father, all things are possible for you: take this cup from me' (Mark 14.36), in other words, spare me this suffering. What suffering? In Matthew and Luke the request sounds rather more modest: 'If it is possible...' And 'If you will . . .' then take this cup from me.

This request of Christ's was not heard by God, his Father. Elsewhere we always find 'I and the Father are one'. Here, however, the communion of Christ with God seems to shatter. So Christ's friends fall into a deep sleep out of sorrow, as though they were paralysed. Christ's unity with the God of his love and his passion is maintained in this divergence only by the 'nevertheless' through which he got control of himself: 'Nevertheless, not my will but your will be done.' Christ's true passion, his suffering over God, begins with his prayer in Gethsemane, which is not heard, but rejected by God's silence. Certainly here too there is simple human fear of pain. It would be brutal to claim that as Son of God Christ could not have felt any fear. But it would also be foolish to regard him as a sensitive weakling who had given way to sentimental self-pity because of physical torment and his imminent death.

I believe that here quite a different fear seized Christ and tore his soul apart: the fear that he, the only Son, who loved the Father as no one had yet loved him, could be 'forsaken' by the Father. He did not fear for his life; he feared for God. He was anxious about the Father's kingdom, the bliss of which he had proclaimed to the poor.

This suffering over God himself is the real torment in Christ's passion. This abandonment by God is the cup which does not pass by him. God's frightful silence to Christ's prayer in Gethsemane is more than a deadly silence. Mystics felt it later in the 'dark night of the soul', in which all that brings life alive dries up, and hope vanishes. Martin Buber called this the 'darkness of God'.

Who can remain awake in this night of God? Who is not virtually paralysed by it? Jesus' friends were spared the terror by deep sleep. Luke, the physician, and other witnesses speak of a 'bloody sweat' which fell to earth from the watching, praying Christ. In the Luther Bible, this chapter is headed 'The Struggle in Gethsemane'. The struggle with whom? Christ's struggle with himself? The struggle with death? I think it is even more than this. It is Christ's struggle with God. That is where his agony lies. He overcame this agony by his surrender. Therein lies his victory and our hope.

2. Golgotha

The other story comes at the end of Christ's passion at Golgotha, the place of execution. Again it is a prayer, or more precisely a desperate cry to God. 'And about the ninth hour Jesus cried out, "My God, my God, why have you forsaken me?"' (Mark 15.34).

For three hours he hung nailed to the cross, evidently silent, waiting for death in cramped agony. And then he died with a cry which expresses the deepest dereliction, the sense of being forsaken by the God on whom he had set all his hope and for whom he was hanging there on the cross. This must be the hard historical core of the story about Golgotha. The idea that the last word of the dying Son to God his Father could be 'You have forsaken me' could never have taken root in Christianity had this fearful saying never been uttered or could not have been heard in the dying cry of Jesus. We will never be able to get used to the fact that at the centre of Christian faith can be heard this cry of the godforsaken Christ to God. Rather, as already happened in the New Testament and then in church history, we shall attempt to tone down its effects and replace it with 'more pious' words of farewell. Nevertheless, terrifying though this dying cry of Christ is, one feels darkly that it is important, indeed vitally necessary, for us. For it is the cry which so many tormented people could join in because it expresses their true situation: 'My God, why have you forsaken me?' Will we too remember Christ if we are forsaken and have to cry out like this?

Nor does this saying become more acceptable by being the beginning of Psalm 22. The idea that the dying Jesus prayed the whole of Psalm 22 on the cross is really bizarre. First, the psalm ends with a splendid prayer of thanksgiving for deliverance from the distress of death, and that did not happen on the cross. Secondly, after only a short time on the cross those who were crucified were incapable of saying anything. No, this is the cry of someone who has been forsaken and cries to the God who has left him in the lurch. Old manuscripts of the Gospel of Mark put it even more strongly: 'Why have you exposed me to shame?' and 'Why have you cursed me?' Even the much later Letter to the Hebrews retains this recollection: 'That far from God [literally, without God] he tasted death for us all' (2.9). And only here on the cross does Christ no longer address God in a familiar way as 'Father', but only officially, as 'God', as though he has to doubt that he is the Son of God the Father.

What Christ feared, what he struggled over in Gethsemane,

what he prayed to the Father for, did not pass, but took place on the cross. The Son bears the judgment in which no one can intercede any longer for others, in which everyone is alone and which no one can withstand.

Is there an answer to the question why God forsook him? The gospel says that it happened 'for us', for you and me, so that we are no longer alone. God gave up his Son 'for us', so that he should be the brother of all the forsaken and bring them to God.

A real answer to the question 'My God, why have you forsaken me?' cannot be a theoretical one, beginning 'Because . . .'. It must be practical. Such an experience cannot be answered by any explanation, but only by another experience; such a reality can only be answered by a new reality. There is really only one answer to the question, 'My God, why have you forsaken me?' That is the resurrection: 'I have abandoned you for a brief moment, but I will gather you with great mercy.' Any other answer would fall short and eternalize death or fail to take it seriously. To this death of the Son, abandoned by God, the only answer is 'Death is swallowed up in victory' (I Cor.15.55). That is Easter.

At the centre of Christian faith stands the story of Christ's passion. At the centre of this passion stands the godforsaken Christ's experience of God. Is this the end of all human and religious hope, or is it the beginning of the true, the reborn hope which nothing can shatter any longer?

The Christ who loves with a passionate love, the persecuted Christ, the lonely Christ, the Christ who suffers over God's silence, the Christ so utterly forsaken in his dying for us and for our sake, is the brother, the friend, to whom one can entrust everything, because he knows everything and has suffered whatever can happen to us – and even more.

3. The giving up of the Son

Paul, with his theology of the giving up of the Son, comes closest to Golgotha. In the Gospels, which depict the death of Jesus in the light of his life and his gospel, 'giving up' has a clearly negative sense. It means 'hand over', 'betray', 'cast out', as can be seen from the description of the 'traitor' Judas. The abandonment of

Jesus by the Father on the cross means his rejection, his being cursed by the Father. Paul also uses the expression 'give up' (Rom.1.18ff.) for God's anger and judgment on human sin. People who forsake the invisible God and worship creatures are forsaken by God and given up to their desires.

Paul makes a radical change to the sense of 'give up' when he no longer sees the abandonment of God by Jesus in the light of his life but in that of his resurrection. The God who has raised Jesus from the dead is the God who has 'given him up' to death on the cross. In the abandonment of the cross itself, from which Jesus cries out 'Why?', Paul already sees the answer to the cry. 'He who did not spare his own Son but gave him up for us all, will he not also give us all things with him?' (Rom.8.32). According to this, the Father has forsaken his 'own Son', as Paul explicitly stresses here, has handed him over and given him up to death. Paul says even more strongly, 'He made him sin for us' (II Cor.5.21) and 'he became a curse for us' (Gal.3.13). The Father forsakes the Son 'for us' in order to become the God and Father of the forsaken. The Father 'gives up' the Son in order through him to become the Father of those who are 'given up' (Rom.1.18ff.). The Son is delivered over to this death to become the brother and saviour of the condemned and the accursed.

The Son suffers death in this forsakenness. The Father suffers the death of the Son. The death of the Son is therefore matched by the grief of the Father. And if the Son loses the Father in this descent into hell, the Father also loses the Son in this judgment. Here the innermost life of the Trinity is involved. Here the love of the Father which communicates itself becomes infinite pain at the sacrifice of the Son. Here the responsive love of the Son becomes infinite suffering over being rejected and cast out by the Father. What happens on Golgotha extends to the depths of the Godhead and therefore shapes the divine life for ever.

According to Gal.2.20, however, the Son is not just given up by the Father. He also 'gave himself up for me'. In the event of giving up he is not only object but also subject. His life and death were an active passion, a way of suffering deliberately embarked on, an affirmative dying. According to the hymn to Christ which Paul takes up in Philippians 2, the self-surrender of the Son consists in his emptying himself of the divine form in his servant form, in his humiliation of himself and the fact that he became 'obedient even to the death on the cross'. For the Letter to the Hebrews (5.8), he 'learned obedience by what he suffered'. Paradoxically, he suffered over the prayer that was not heard, over being forsaken by the Father. By that he 'learned' obedience and self-surrender. That corresponds to the Synoptic account of the passion story.

In theological terms this primarily represents an inner communion of will between the Son who is given up and the will of the Father to give him up. That is also the content of the Gethsemane story. Now this deep communion of will comes into being precisely at the point of the furthest separation of the Son from the Father and the Father from the Son, in the accursed death on the cross, in the 'dark night' of this death. On the cross the Son and the Father are so separated that their relationship threatens to be broken. Jesus dies 'God-less'. On the cross the Father and the Son are at the same time so at one that they represent a single movement of self-surrender: 'Whoever sees the Son sees the Father.' The Letter to the Hebrews expresses that by saying that Christ sacrificed himself to God 'through the eternal Spirit' (9.14). The giving up by the Father and the sacrifice of the Son happen 'through the Spirit'. So the Holy Spirit is what holds them together in the separation, what forms both the bond and the separation of the Father and the Son from one another.

Paul explained the event of the godforsakenness on the cross as the giving up of the Son, and the giving up of the Son as the love of God. What the love of God is, 'from which nothing can separate us' (Rom.8.39), took place on the cross and is experienced on the cross. In his Son, the Father who sends the Son through all the abysses and hells of godforsakenness, the curse of God and the final judgment, is everywhere among his own; he is omnipresent. In giving up the Son he gives everything, and nothing can separate us from him. That is the beginning of talk of the kingdom of God, in which God will be all in all. Anyone who recognizes the presence and love of God in the godforsakenness of the crucified Son will see God in all things, just as after an experience of death someone will sense the life in all things in a previously unsuspected way.

The Gospel of John summarizes the giving up in the sentence, 'God so loved the world that he gave his only begotten Son that all who believe in him should not perish but have everlasting life' (3.16). The 'so' means 'in this way': in the dereliction suffered 'for us' in the death on the cross. And I John defines God here as 'God is love' (4.16); God does not merely love, just as at one point he is angry. He *is* love. His being is love. He constitutes himself as love. That took place on the cross. This definition takes on its full importance only if one constantly keeps in mind the way to it: the dereliction of Jesus on the cross, the giving up of the Son by the Father and the love which does all, gives all, endures all for lost human beings. God is love, i.e. God is giving-up, i.e. God exists for us – on the cross.

4. Is God impassible or does God suffer?

If we ask what is appropriate for God in terms of Greek philosophy, then we have to exclude difference, variety, movement and suffering from the being of the Godhead. The divine substance is incapable of suffering; otherwise it would not be divine. The absolute subject of nominalist and idealist philosophy is also incapable of suffering; otherwise it would not be absolute. Impassible, immovable, one and self-sufficient, the Godhead stands over against a moved, suffering, dispersed world which is never self-sufficient. For the divine substance is what grounds, supports and remains eternal for this world of transitory phenomena and therefore cannot be subject to the fate of this world.

However, if one asks the same question in terms of the theological proclamation of the Christian tradition, one finds at its centre the story of Christ's passion. The suffering and death of Christ are related in the gospel. The giving up of the Son of God for the redemption of the world is communicated in the eucharist in the form of bread and wine. Through the representation of the passion of Christ in word and sacrament faith is called forth, Christian faith in God. Those who believe owe their freedom to Christ, their representative. Because of Christ they believe in God. God himself is involved in the story of Christ's passion, otherwise the death of Christ could have no redemptive effect. But in what way is God himself involved in the story of Christ's passion? How can Christian faith understand the passion of Christ as the revelation of God if the Godhead cannot suffer? Does God make Christ suffer for us, or does God himself suffer in Christ for us?

Since the development of Christian theology in the thought-forms of Greek philosophy, in Hellenistic culture, most theologians have simultaneously maintained both the passion of Christ, the Son of God, and the essential impassibility of the Godhead, and thus created the paradox of having to talk in terms of the 'suffering of the God who is incapable of suffering'. In so doing, however, they have simply added together the axiom of impassibility, *apatheia*, from Greek philosophy and the central statements of the gospel. The contradiction remains, and remains unsatisfactory.

Up to the present the axiom of impassibility has stamped the basic concepts of the doctrine of God more strongly than the story of Christ's passion. Impassibility is evidently regarded as an indispensable attribute of divine perfection and bliss. But does this not mean that up to the present Christian theology has failed to develop a consistent Christian concept of God, and for reasons which are still to be investigated has tended more to borrow from the metaphysical tradition of Greek philosophy which it understood as 'natural theology' and regarded as its foundation?

The more strongly the axiom of impassibility is heeded in the doctrine of God, the weaker becomes the capacity of that doctrine to identify God with the passion of Christ. If God is impassible, then it is logical to regard the passion of Christ as a merely human tragedy. But to anyone who can see no more in the passion of Christ than the suffering of the good man from Nazareth, God must inexorably become the cold, silent and unloved heavenly power. That would be the end of Christian faith.

Christian theology is therefore in essence compelled to recognize God himself in Christ's passion and to discover Christ's passion in God himself. Given the numerous attempts to mediate christologically between impassibility and passion in such a way as to maintain the axiom of impassibility, it seems to be more consistent to start from the axiom of the suffering of God rather than from the axiom of impassibility, in order to understand the passion of Christ as the passion of the God who is capable of passion. The word 'passion' has the twofold meaning of suffering and being passionate, and is therefore well suited in this twofold significance to express the central truth of Christian faith. Christian faith lives by the suffering of a great passion and is itself a passion for life which is ready to suffer. But why did the early church hold on to the axiom of impassibility in its theology, although Christian piety worshipped the crucified Christ as God and Christian preaching could speak of the 'suffering of God'?

Two reasons can be given for this.

1. God's essential impassibility distinguishes him from human beings and all things that are not God, who are subject to suffering, as they are to transitoriness and death.

2. If God gives men and women salvation by giving them a share in his eternal life, then this salvation brings people immortality, permanence, and therefore also impassibility.

So impassibility is the divine being and the embodiment of human salvation in the divine community.

The logical limitation of this argument is that it recognizes only two alternatives: essential impassibility on the one hand or subjection to suffering through fate on the other. But there is a third form of suffering: active suffering, voluntarily becoming open to being affected by others, i.e. the passion of passionate love. In Christian theology the axiom of impassibility really conveys only that God is not subject to suffering in the same way as the transitory creation. Thus it is not a real axiom but a comparison. It does not exclude the possibility that in another respect God may very well suffer and indeed does suffer. Were God impassible in every respect, he would also be incapable of love. At any rate, he would be capable of loving himself, but not of loving other than himself, as Aristotle says. But if God is capable of loving other things, then he opens himself to the suffering which the love of others brings him, and remains above the pain which arises as a result, but by virtue of his love. God does not suffer, as does creation, from lack of being. To this degree he is impassible. But he suffers through his love which is the superfluity of his being. To that degree he is capable of suffering.

Probably only Origen in the early church recognized and used this distinction. He is the only one among the Greek and Latin church fathers to venture to speak theologically of the 'suffering of God'.

God suffers in his mercy; so he is not without a heart.

He (the Redeemer) came down to earth out of compassion for the human race. He suffered our suffering before he endured the cross and before he deigned to assume our flesh; for had he not suffered (beforehand), he would not have entered into the changes of human life. First he suffered, then he descended and became visible. What kind of a suffering is it that he suffered for us? Love is suffering (*Caritas est passio*). And does not the Father himself, the God of the universe, 'longsuffering and of great mercy' (Ps.103.8), suffer in the same way? Or do you not know that when he descends to humankind he suffers human suffering? 'The Lord your God bore you, as a man bears his son' (Deut.1.31). So God bears us, as the Son of God bears our suffering. Even the Father is not incapable of suffering (*Ipse pater non est impassibilis*). When he is called on, he has mercy and also feels our grief. He suffers a suffering of love and becomes something that he cannot be because of the magnitude of his nature, and for our sakes bears human suffering.

When Origen speaks of the suffering of God, he means the suffering of love, the sympathy which lies in the nature of mercy. Those who are merciful take part in the suffering of others, take other suffering upon themselves, suffer for others. For Origen, this suffering is divine suffering. It is the suffering of God who bears the world by bearing its burden. It is the suffering of the Father who in giving up his 'own Son' (Rom.8.32) suffers the pain of redemption. It is the suffering of the Son of God who takes upon himself our sins and sicknesses. So Origen speaks of a divine passion which Christ endures for us, and at the same time points to a divine passion which takes place between the Father and the Son in the Trinity. For the divine suffering of love outside is grounded in the pain of love within.

5. The comfort of the Crucified

At the centre of the biblical traditions stand the story of the passion of Israel and the story of the passion of Jesus Christ. The

God who led Israel to freedom and made his covenant with this people is not an impassible God, but a God with the passion and the zeal of love. So in the passion story of their people the rabbis constantly also discovered the passion story of the God of Israel. As 'the Almighty', God is enthroned in heaven, but by virtue of his spirit he is at the same time in and with his people; he is particularly close to the poor and the humiliated, to widows and orphans. God is present in Israel through his Shekinah (indwelling); he suffers in the persecution of his followers, he goes into exile with the people and shares the torments of death with the martyrs. The God of the covenant is also Israel's companion in suffering. This experience of the pain and suffering of God in his own was and is the inexhaustible power which preserves the people from despair and keeps their disappointed hope alive.

Christians have recognized and believed something similar in the story of the passion of Jesus Christ. The sufferings of Christ are the sufferings of God himself. God himself becomes human. God himself becomes this person and enters into the passion of the cross on Golgotha. God assumes this humanity and embraces it with his divine being. God assumes the situation of the godforsakeness of lost men and women and takes their death on himself. This human God is near to all human beings in their dereliction. Women and men are unconditionally accepted into the community of God wherever they are. There is nothing that could exclude them from the community of the human, crucified God.

Jews and Christians can speak of the pain and suffering of God and in their own suffering and pain experience deep inner communion with God because they believe in the God who is merciful. The God whose being is love goes out from himself by virtue of his love. His love for his creation and the human beings whom he has created in his image causes him suffering. He suffers in the contradictions of his creatures, he suffers in being shut out by his creatures and he suffers for his creatures in infinite patience, because he keeps hoping for the free conversion and grateful homecoming of his creatures. So God in his love is omnipotent and at the same time impotent. His love triumphs in hope and suffers in patient waiting.

What does this God mean for people who suffer and have to look on suffering?

Those who suffer without reason always begin by thinking that they have been forsaken by God and all that is good. Those who cry out to God in their suffering in essence join in Jesus' dying cry, 'My God, why have you forsaken me?'. When they recognize this, they also recognize that God is not that dark adversary in heaven to whom they cry, but in a very personal sense is the human brother who cries with them and the Spirit which cries in them and will cry for them when they are put to silence.

It is said that Catherine of Siena once cried out: 'Where were you, my God and Lord, when my heart was full of darkness and confusion?' And she heard the answer, 'I was in your heart, my dear daughter.'

For me the Christ who is solitary, forsaken, assailed and made anxious is in a very personal sense the proof of the solidarity of God in suffering. If we look at the cross from outside, detached from the experience of our own suffering, we can already ask what kind of a Father it is who sits enthroned in heaven and allows his own Son to come to so miserable an end on earth. The gruesome image can then arise of a divine sadist who looks on at such torment of his 'beloved Son' and does not intervene. But if we look more closely, then we recognize the Father *in* the Son. 'He who sees me,' says Jesus according to the Gospel of John, 'sees the Father' (14.9). For Paul, 'God himself was in Christ reconciling the world to himself' (II Cor.5.19), and by 'God' Paul always means 'the Father of Jesus Christ'. So where the Son goes, there the Father goes with him, and when the Son suffers, then the Father suffers with him – not in the same way as the Son but in his own way. So we cannot say that God killed his own Son or caused him to suffer. On the contrary; God himself suffered this death of his beloved child and shared his grief. The god in whose name Jesus was crucified by the Romans is called Jupiter, not Yahweh nor Abba, Jesus's name for God. Jupiter is certainly also a father god or a father of the gods, but he is one who calls for sacrifices which people are to bring him in order to put him in a peaceful and caring mood, not one who sacrifices himself in order to show solidarity with the forsaken and the suffering and to reconcile himself with them. Only at the beginning of Christendom, under the emperor Constantine, were the Roman Jupiter and Jesus' Hebrew 'Abba' fused into a single image of God. Many problems with the theology of the cross which are produced by some feminist theologians today arise from this fusion. Nevertheless, the difference is easy to recognize: Abba, the Father of Jesus, stands on the side of the crucified Christ; Jupiter stands against him.[1]

There is a Jewish story which can help us to understand the 'compassionate God':

> When the Holy One, Blessed be He, comes to free the children of Israel from exile, they will say to Him: Lord of the world, it was you who scattered us among the nations by driving us from our homeland, and now are you going to take us back there again? And the Holy One, Blessed be He, said to the children of Israel: When I saw that you had left my homeland, I also left it, to come back with you.

On this Elie Wiesel writes: 'God accompanies his children into exile: this theme dominates the thought-world of the Midrash and mysticism in the Jewish tradition.'[2]

Is there a feminist theology of the cross?

Elisabeth Moltmann-Wendel

Nowadays the cross, the most important symbol in Christianity, has become a problem for many women. The tortured body of Christ on the cross and his death – interpreted as an atoning death – no longer give them any strength. A Swiss woman theological student made a brief, ironic comment on the Christian cross: 'I'm not hanging any guillotine round my neck!' A woman suffering from cancer expressed what many people feel: 'The crucified Christ no longer says anything to me, but the picture of Mary with the child radiates comfort and security for me.'

The cross as it is often preached has often had fatal consequences for women. 'Taking up one's cross' could mean patiently tolerating a violent husband, social injustice and other wrongs that need to be remedied. Such preaching of the cross could contribute to keeping women down and oppressing them. 'Crucifying the flesh' has usually been understood as the renunciation of pleasure and joy, and as crucifying the desires.

Can a history of the cross with such effects be rescued? What significance can the story of the crucifixion of Jesus and the cross as a symbol regain for women? These questions have bothered me for a long time in the face of a feminist theology which is again outraged at the theology of the cross. This outrage is also reinforced by the antipathy to a necrophilic symbol expressed by other psychological and religious camps. It receives support from Jewish Christian groups who do not see the crucifixion of Jesus as anything special, but rather as an instance of a capital punishment which was often inflicted in the Roman Empire, thereby putting in question the Christian claim to the uniqueness of Jesus and the significance of the crucifixion. So we have a massive criticism of the central symbol of Christianity not only among women but above all among women from a group which has hitherto been silent in the church, which has a new psychological and social understanding of itself. The criticism – and this seems to me to be important – is a religious criticism which is at the same time a criticism of patriarchal thought-patterns. Will feminist theology become a theology without the cross? What presuppositions underlie this? What repudiation of patriarchal notions is justified? And what content remains?

I

First I would like to say something about the approach of feminist theology in contrast to that of traditional theology:

Feminist theology begins from experiences and not from the revelation event.

It begins especially from the social experiences of women, the discrimination against them and their invisibility in male-dominated societies and churches.

It points out that women and men are shaped by other psychological and social presuppositions which then in turn also shape their images of themselves, the world and God.

In the meantime, as a result of the works of Carol Gilligan and Anne Wilson Schaef,[3] we have come to learn the difference between masculine and feminine thought-patterns. However, we should not in any way understand these different thought-patterns as eternal modes of being, but regard them as being above all socially conditioned. Most of our current theological ideas are strongly stamped by masculine patterns of thought and life. When women understand this, they find it easier to see traditional theology as an expression of such a view of self and the world, rather than accusing it of being destructive or necrophilic. Such psychological and social analyses seem to me to be the only chance of entering into a critical dialogue. From this point I want to attempt to get closer to the conflicts over the theology of the cross.

The theology of the cross as it has now fallen into disrepute contains some typical elements of the male picture of man and the world. I can only make a few points here, briefly and over-simplifying. In leaving the sphere of the mother, the feminine, the world of the feelings and an initial security, to enter a male society and have to assert himself in this society through achievements, a man may perhaps be in conflict all his life: guilty at having abandoned his origins and having – with hybris – to attain high ideals, e.g. equality with God. This is the sin which Kierkegaard describes as despair at wanting to be oneself.[4] These primal experiences are matched in theology. The Abrahamic religions with their approach from the need to depart from the father's house have legitimated the secret contempt for origins and the forward pressure towards future fulfilment. To become a man it is necessary to leave one's origins, but that brings a feeling of guilt; it can be experienced as godlessness, since the goal is unattainable. As Anne Wilson Schaef sees it, 'In the White Male System, living in tune with God means getting in tune with something outside the self... In order to be attuned to God, then, one must learn to deny or transcend the self. One must strive to be what one is not' (168).

In my view, sin as an expression of distance from God thus has its central place in the male system, as the experience of incompetence and helplessness, the fundamental alienation from God and other human beings. The one who is God-less is a frequent theme of theology and the starting point for the theology of the cross.

In the Female System, by contrast, Wilson Schaef argues, 'living in tune with god means being in tune with what one already *is*'. Anyone who is in harmony with her own process is also in harmony with God. 'And god is not *just* our process and God *is* our process . . .' (ibid). 'When we are out of tune with our internal process, though, we distort ourselves and are often destructive to others. That is the real nature of sin' (ibid.). One does not despair of wanting to be oneself – Kierkegaard's other sin is more in accord with women's experience.

The themes of feminist theology – the search for Goddess as the principle which is friendly to life, for a feminine God-ness, the motherly God or process theology – are an expression of this feminine system, this distinctive way to theological self-determination.

If we make a list of the conceptions of God in the two systems, we get the following result:

In the male system God is above all a person and a secret pattern for identification. He is thought of as being outside this world and is the goal of one's being.

By contrast, in the feminine system God is seen above all as a power of life, less personal and more transpersonal, and as a power of relationship. God/Goddess is named and experienced within the world and is an experience of origin and permanent power of relationship – like life itself.

At present, the two systems stand over against each other as absolutes, and the reciprocal attacks end up in suspicions of a 'Fascist religion of origins' or a 'necrophilic religion'.

This rough list helps me to understand male and also female theological approaches better, and at the same time also to see them critically. Where has masculine theology distorted the passion stories with its principle of sins? Where does women's theology attempt to trap God/Goddess in an immanent system and to skirt the fringes of the passion?

I want to go on from here in the second part to give an account of the feminist critiques of the theology of the cross and at the same time of my own criticism of the feminist critique of the cross. In the third part I shall outline the possibilities for a feminist theology of the cross.

II

A criticism of critiques of the cross

So far the charges against the theology of the cross are unresolved. I want to see them in the context of male thought and at the same time ask how far they are justified.

1. Sado-masochism

Obviously God as person and also as a secret figure with whom to identify stands at the centre of the masculine theology of the cross. This image of God has been attacked by women. Feminist theology seems no longer able to tolerate a God who according to Paul's testimony in the Bible has *given up* (Rom.8.32) his Son. Comparisons are made with Himmler. Women have said that this attitude of God's and of the men who interpret it is sado-masochism. At the same time, however, what they have proclaimed as 'men's theology' is also a defamatory distortion. For example, Elga Sorge presents Gollwitzer as having said that God had his Son 'murdered' instead of 'killed'. She then concludes from this: '. . . The traditional image of God encourages an attitude of faith which is orientated more on suffering, torture and violence than on love, pleasure and joy', without perceiving the mysterious surrender, God's *allowing* or permitting, which is Gollwitzer's point.[5]

This surrender plays a central role in both the New Testament and the theological tradition. It is passion terminology, for two thousand years burdened with and trapped in male experiences of themselves and the world, above all with experiences of helplessness. The notion surfaces in the New Testament. In the Gospels it is Judas, the one who betrays Jesus, who is handed over. But in Paul, God himself already seems to have become the agent. This interpretation is then developed fully in Christian piety, in hymns and so on. God can appear as an incomprehensible, cruel Father who by the abandonment and death of his Son needs satisfaction for insults caused by human alienation. Unfortunately the Pauline version won out over the Synoptic version. But strictly speaking *paradidonai* contains something of the enigmatic character of this event: a human being, Judas, was the agent, but if God has all the power in his hands, then in an enigmatic way he is also involved.

We should detect in the protest of the women that the theology of the cross should not just be coupled to a personal image of God which can give the impression of a God who acts in a sadistic way. It should allow the *paradidonai* to stand, or return to the statements of the Gospels that a human being handed Jesus over.

In connection with reflections on Auschwitz, in recent years images of the pain of God have been rediscovered. They protect male theology from getting a grip on the enigma of God. They teach us to maintain it and not to resolve it cheaply.

However, a God who is only pleasure, love and joy, and the promise of a Jesus-like happiness which sometimes emerges, arouses in me the suspicion which Barbara Sichtermann once critically noted in connection with feminist notions of sexuality, which she call 'cup-a-soup sexuality': an all-too-easy agreement of bodies in an exchange of affirmations. Is there not in normal sexuality, she asked, some sado-masochism, the giving and enduring of pain, an element from the figure of the dance, initially independent of gender and only by cultural definitions split into feminine here and masculine there? In every pleasure there is a pain, a little death. Without passion there is no ecstasy.[6]

A kind of 'cup-a-soup God' keeps cropping up in the quest of feminist theology for life. This God cannot do justice to us as whole persons and forces us into niches which no longer match reality. I can also rediscover the figures of the dance, of which Barbara Sichtermann speaks, in the old ideas of the perichoretic dance in the Trinity and the new ones which have been discovered today.

2. The cross as a legitimation of force

Women have now sometimes replaced the unpopular theology of the cross with a Jesus who has been domesticated in line with their own ideas. They have de-crucified Jesus.

In contrast to the theology of the cross, Maria Kassel, for example, develops her own conception of death and resurrection from a feminine context, using the myth of Inanna's journey into the underworld.[7] In it she discovers a 'creative, birthing feminine death, the goddess death'. The message of the myth is then: 'The suffering of birth and the blood which is naturally poured out with it redeems life from death . . . The fate of the dead goddess of life hanging on the tree who at the same time gives birth as the goddess of death' needs 'no justification from a theology of sins'. For many women – including myself – this image is very attractive, in that it depicts the process of human life, letting go and becoming new, takes the experience of death into life, interprets death existentially and frees us from rigid patriarchal patterns of life.

However, the critical comment has to be made that this is a mythological image which hardly has any connection with the notion of the cross. Two essential elements of the story of the cross as it is told in the New Testament are missing. Maria Kassel has quite deliberately overlooked one of them, the violence of the death of Jesus. Kassel wants the Christian theology of the cross 'for the salvation of human beings and the world' once again to take up the symbols of non-violent suffering and dying. Here, however, she has failed to note an important cornerstone in the theology of the cross: the brutal power of the state which destroyed Jesus as an enemy of the state. Without this aspect, a theology of the cross is a help only to individual living and dying.

In such a mythological reinterpretation of the cross – helpful though it may be in coping with existence – the personal and political significance of the story of Jesus can no longer be recognized.

The second forgotten element is just as important: the dereliction of Jesus expressed in the cry 'My God, why have you forsaken me?' I find it striking that this cry hardly ever appears in women's accounts. For example, Carter Heyward cannot imagine the anger of Jesus as anger against God. She talks of an 'exception'.[8] In this cry it becomes clear to her that Jesus finally and fully recognized 'the price of relationship'. 'The wrath of Jesus' was not diffuse or unconcentrated. The wrath of Jesus had a particular focus: 'the non-relationship, the broken relationship, the violated relationship, the destruction of God in the world. . .' This interpretation seems to me to be mistaken, since there is no insight in this cry of dereliction from Jesus! It is an expression of the most helpless dereliction. It is an elemental cry without purpose and aim. The question is, may there no longer be any despair in feminist theology? Has a harmonious feminine religious solution done away with all anxieties?

I find a similar reinterpretation, which takes the edge of this dereliction, in Rita Nakashima Brock, when she writes: 'Jesus does not die totally abandoned, though he is described as feeling godforsaken. The divine erotic power illuminated through Christa/Community in Galilee and the woman at Bethany is sustained through Jesus' death by those who watch him die and mark his burial site.'

But the New Testmaent makes a distinction between godforsakenness and being forsaken by human beings. It describes the presence of the women, but this cannot remove the godforsakenness. The godforsakenness of Jesus remains the riddle which I simply cannot reinterpret. There is godforsakenness which cannot be done away with by any erotic power or power of relationship. We cannot simply reduce experiences of God to human experiences. 'Were "God" only a title for the event of interpersonal love, what could be said to the one who is abandoned by all people and all love? The tautology between God and the event of interpersonal love is done away with by the gospel of God's love' (H.Gollwitzer).[10]

3. The cross as the cause of an ethic of subjection

In the meantime, critiques of the cross have extended to questions of soteriology, ethics and exegesis, and now culminate in the question put by a Swiss theologian, Regula Strobel: 'How can we think of the act of violence, the judicial murder of Jesus, in connection with the theological concept of redemption? On the basis of what experience are we to see our redemption specifically in the crucifixion of Jesus?... Can such a repressive, bloody act ever bring redemption, salvation and blessing?'[11]

Strobel's presuppositions for the traditional theology of the cross are:

1. The general sinfulness of human beings:
2. God and human beings as counterparts;
3. Human impotence to make good.

Therefore a bloody human sacrifice has to be justified, which for her has catastrophic consequences in ethics both old and new: looking for scapegoats for social disasters (persecution of witches, Jews and so on); human injustice (e.g. bombing in El Salvador) in order to stylize the saving action of God. An ethic of obedience and subjection then amounts to following the attitude of Jesus. The values mediated with the cross and the theology of the cross have thus stabilized oppression.

The conclusion from these general considerations which can be derived above all from the history of the effect of the cross is that Jesus redeems by his life and action and not by his death. People should again rely on just action in solidarity, restraint and love, the development and requirement of which could be our redemption and the redemption of the world. Redemption does not take place through an objective act of salvation – what happens on the cross – but in the continuation of the healing activity of Jesus in human mutuality. The presupposition of this concept is the immediacy of God and human beings as it is expressed in the experience of women: to be oneself is to be with God.

To interpret the cross only as an atoning sacrifice is to restrict theology. Here feminist theology is right. There is a need to give a new theological foundation to an ethics of reciprocity. The question remains whether this is possible only in the limited form of the life of Jesus, and whether human redemptive action is already redemption.

From this perspective, Christian theology is reduced to a moral action with the highest claims; redemptive action is put in the hands of human beings themselves.

To sum up, it has to be said:

All three theological outlines presented here are reactions to violence suffered personally and socially. They attempt to develop a gentle theology of non-violence and a utopia of feasible, achievable happiness. They attempt to grasp God in immanence, in the process of life and an ethic of reciprocity. Men and women are activated, ethics replaces dogmatics – the problem is whether as a result a religion of the nearness of God without the terror of God is dreamed up, a human picture of strength, will and divine immanence which passes over our abysses and God's riddles. I think that even the power of relationship can break. Even Jesus broke on it. Even this Godhead/Goddess can die. God is not just in our forces, open and hidden, nor just in our solidarity, nor just in our will to life or our lifeblood. God is also there. But he is not only there.

The women's concept of an absolutely non-violent religion must ask itself whether it is overlooking reality in its dreams and taking refuge in a life-of-Jesus religion without perceiving the death of Jesus, and whether, remote from all criticism of religion, it is creating a transpersonal image of God as a power of life which no longer allows any paradox.

However, in view of this massive feminist critique we must ask whether the violence experienced in male socialization (detachment from the mother, from the origin, from the feminine sphere) does not perhaps makes it too natural to accept and to integrate violence. To what degree does the theology of the cross reflect a degree of male individuation which many women have also had to copy? And has not Adorno grasped something of this 'cross' when he writes: 'Humanity has had to do fearful things to itself in order that the self, the identical, purpose-orientated, male man, the male character of man, should be created, and something of that is still repeated in every childhood'? Traditional theology has to ask itself whether its one-sided personal image of God has not sanctioned God as the agent in world history who is responsible for everything and therefore cruel, even to the extent of a personal experience of violence.

III

A feminist theology of the cross

How can the passion for immanence which arises among women from so much suffering be preserved without bracketting out the passion story?

Is there now a feminist theology of the cross? I think that there is, but it must be embedded in a christology and an account of Jesus in which it is not just Jesus' 'work' – in parallel to the male's life-work – that makes up salvation history, as is the case with so many traditional outlines from Paul to the present, but his whole life. In the masculine self-understanding person and work are important, but in the feminine understanding so too is the network of relationships, the effect of people. So there is a need to look at this network of relationships from which Jesus lived and which make up his life work, as well as at his death and resurrection.[12] For example, the healing stories in which he healed and was healed are as much part of this work as his political murder. However, the cross may no longer overshadow the healings. When that happens, the 'for me', 'for us' can turn into a historical and spatial 'before me': I can live in his history and the protection it provides.

I can see three feminist dimensions of the cross which do not reduce the cross to the principle of the forgiveness of sins and in which women can involve themselves existentially.

1. The cross as solidarity in suffering
The New Testament story of the cross has two sides. On the one

– 86 –

hand is the story of the guilt of the disciples who fled. On the other is the story of the solidarity of the women who remained under the cross. The latter has so far usually been overlooked. Two or three women remained under the cross who – unlike the disciples – had not fled. Despite the danger to life and limb, they remained at the place of execution, were present at the death and burial of Jesus, and became the first witneses to the resurrection. They stayed under the cross out of solidarity and compassion. In contrast to the disciples, for whom the betrayal and guilt, the feeling of having abandoned Jesus, was the starting point of their experiences of God, for the women the cross is the place of communion with their friend in his sufferings. At the same time it represents detachment from family, custom and social status. It amounts to social death, and brings them the danger of physical death.

For them the cross is not the contradiction of their images of God and their expectations of life. Their own experiences of helplessness are reflected here, their own knowledge of the meaning and the power of solidarity.

I regard this tacit counter-theology from the Gospels as a theology of the cross which we should develop further. Elisabeth Schüssler-Fiorenza has pointed out that the statements about these women at the cross, that they followed Jesus, served him and went up to Jerusalem with him, mark them out as the real disciples. They *serve*, as Jesus himself came to serve and to give his life. This statement is never made about the disciples who were in love with success.[13]

Here the feminist theology of the cross meets up with the last thoughts of Bonhoeffer, from his cell. For him what is now important is not the individual in his search for freedom, nor the Christian come of age, not the 'religious act', but 'participation in the suffering of God' in the life of the world or 'participation in the suffering of God in Christ'.[14] The New Testament instances of this which he cites also include the women in the passion story. For him the question of Jesus in Gethsemane, 'Could you not watch with me one hour?', becomes important as the 'reversal of all that the religious person expects of God'. But the biblical answer is really only that watching is impossible. Bonhoeffer has not yet realized that in the story of the women, in the theological tradition of the women, the image of the women who watch with Jesus in Gethsemane, there is a starting point for the tradition of the women in the passion stories. It was not seen at that time that there are subversive traditions with other answers than the reaction of the disciples – sleep.[15]

The individual male experience and knowledge behind such statements about participation in the suffering of God are perhaps different from those of women. Whereas Bonhoeffer says, 'Christians stand by God in his suffering', it is more natural for women today to say, 'Where people suffer, Christ suffers with them.' Here I see differences that are specific to tradition and sex, but which for me are not opposites. They are two sides of the same coin, pointing to different expressions of theological culture which are not just gender-specific. They should not separate us, but invite us to dialogue.

2. The cross as suffering from structural sin

Alongside the tradition of the cross as solidarity with those who suffer there is another women's tradition down the centuries: the image of the crucified woman. This type of image comes from the saga of the father who wanted to marry his daughter to a pagan; when she refused, in his fury he had her crucified. At the present time, pictures of crucified women have appeared in many countries and cultures as a reflection of women's reality. They can shock both women, who find in them only a reflection of their own humiliation, without drawing strength and identity from them, and men, who see them as blasphemy. I lectured to women theologians in a church in Korea under the giant picture of a crucified Asian woman. For a long time a crucified 'Christa' by Edwina Sandys, the British artist, was in the Women's Center in Berkeley and provoked a wealth of reflections and reactions. In its vulnerability and nakedness women saw themselves as objects of forbidden pleasure, as anorexic and self-scorning, as those who could no longer develop any creativity and spirituality from themselves and their bodies. Men saw their Jewish mothers weeping over Auschwitz. They also saw their own feminine aspects crucified and destroyed. Remarkably, here this image of the crucifixion was not felt to be destructive, but a way from death to life.

In her book *Transforming Grace*, the American feminist theologian Anne Carr has called the cross 'a central Christian symbol and an important one for Christian women who experience the pain of exclusion and denigration in their own religious heritage'.[16]

3. *The cross as a paradoxical symbol of life*

If many women nowadays reject the cross as a symbol of the forgiveness of sins, the question remains, is this a women's sin? In what feminine context of life is it represented? And is there a healing (forgiving) symbolism for it?

For me, the passion stories have always been a help in recognizing in our theological thought-patterns gender-specific situations and modes of behaviour from which gender-specific ideas then arise. The end of the Gospel of Mark illustrates this problem for me. Whereas the disciples fled on the arrest of Jesus, the women fled full of terror at the message of the resurrection (Mark 16.8). Whereas the disciples fled in fear of losing their life, and disappointed at the failure of their aims, the women fled when their world shattered, as the result of an invasion from outside, when their network of relationships tore and they no longer had the dead person as the object of their concern and love. They fled when their immanence had holes made in it through the experience of transcendence, when their 'power of relationship' was put in question.

'They have taken away my Lord and I do not know where they have laid him' is Mary Magdalene's lament in the Gospel of John. 'Why do you seek the living among the dead?' is the question of the angels to the women in Matthew.

There are two strident statements in the New Testament, in Mark, which are already harmonized in the later Gospels: Jesus' cry of dereliction on the cross and the flight of the women on Easter morning. They belong in the earliest Christian history. They cannot be harmonized, and they give us a glimpse into abysses. They cannot be removed morally. They belong to the dark side of God and the dark night of the soul, without which the Christian religion, including feminist theology, is in danger of descending to a programme of psychological health or plans to change the world.

In this story of the flight of the women I see parallels to the experiences of many women: they despair when their networks of relationships tear apart. They can give up everything, but this world of surrender, of work to do, must hold. They can remain trapped in the helper syndrome, even the syndrome of helping God. Not to be able to bear the loss of love – that is godforsakenness which prevents people from entering into new spheres independently, upright and alone. Perhaps there is a human quest for love and life which does not come to grief on the solidarity of the cross but on the capacity for resurrection. Perhaps the search for symbols of resurrection is also a problem for humanity that we are learning to express today.

If Western theology is fixed on the cross as its real field of conflict, the unbelievable resurrection, the incursion of another world into a network of feminine relationships which is apparently so intact, seems to be women's real field of conflict.

Women can come to grief on the resurrection, just as the disciples came to grief on the cross. But they can also experience resurrection: by growing out of their narrow, comprehensible, limited world; by letting go of traditional feminine patterns of life; by coming out of themselves and entering into an experience of transcendence which at the same time is immanent, which extends from the narrow feminine sphere into a cosmic and social sphere. This is the message which John's Mary Magdalene experiences in her encounter with the risen Christ: 'Do not touch me.' She must and may be herself. The resurrection brings the pain and grief of becoming a self and entering into new relationships with the world.

Feminist theology, which starts not from a general but from a differentiated understanding of sin, can no longer see the cross in isolation nor just as the symbol of the forgiveness of sins. The cross and the history of the cross can be interpreted in different ways. However, they must no longer just be fixed on a Western patriarchal context, but be extended to new conceptions of life in which the crosses of the world become oppressive. Women nowadays are pointing out how deadly and paralysing a wrong understanding of the cross can be, and with their protest they are calling attention to long-forgotten dimensions of the cross.

In the last resort the cross is a paradoxical symbol. This insight is strengthened by research into symbols: the cross is not just the guillotine or the gallows. Sub-consciously it is also the symbol of totality and life, and probably was able to survive as the central Christian symbol only with what was at the same time a sub-conscious significance. Remnants of it are still preserved in the Celtic cross, the old symbol of life; in depictions of the cross which at the same time portay the tree of life; and in the symbol of Lutheran theology: the rose in the cross of the present.

Perhaps we shall again be able to see the paradox of this symbol one day when the cross is liberated from one-dimensional male experience and is understood anew from the experiences of many people, above all women, experiences which are then not just gender-specific as society changes. Perhaps then we shall see the cross as a symbol of solidarity, as the representation of human suffering, new dimensions of which can always be uncovered, and a sign of salvation that we can erect out of death and nothingness and transplant into new spheres.

Notes

1. For further study of these questions see Jürgen Moltmann, *The Crucified God*, SCM Press and Harper and Row 1974; *The Way of Jesus Christ*, SCM Press and Harper and Row 1990; *History and the Triune God*, SCM Press and Crossroad Publishing Company, 1992.

2. E. Wiesel, 'Der Mitleidende', in R. Walter (ed.), *Die hundert Namen Gottes*, Freiburg 1985, 70.

3. Carol Gilligan, *In a Different Voice: Psychological Theory and Women's Development*, Harvard University Press 1982; Anne Wilson Schaef, *Women's Reality: An Emerging Female System in a White Male Society*, Harper and Row 1985.

4. Søren Kierkegaard, *The Sickness unto Death*.

5. Elga Sorge, *Religion und Frau*, Stuttgart 1985, 43f.

6. Barbara Sichtermann, 'Vergewaltigung und Sexualität', in Marie-louise Janssen-Jurreit, *Frauen und Sexmoral*, Frankfurt 1986, 382ff.

7. Maria Kassel, 'Tod und Auferstehung', in id., *Feministische Theologie. Perspektiven zur Orientierung*, Stuttgart 1988, 212.

8. Carter Heyward, *Our Passion for Justice: Images of Power, Sexuality and Liberation*, Pilgrim Press 1984, 105f.

9. Rita Nakashima Brock, *Journeys by Heart. A Christology of Erotic Power*, Crossroad Publishing Company 1988, 98.

10. Helmut Gollwitzer, *Von der Stellvertretung Gottes. Christlicher Glaube in der Erfahrung der Verborgenheit Gottes*, Munich 1967, 147.

11. Regula Strobel, 'Wollte Gott uns durch Blut erlösen?', Stuttgart lecture, 12 March 1990.

12. There is more on this in E. Moltmann-Wendel, *Weiblichkeit in der Theologie. Verdrängung und Wiederkehr*, Gütersloh 1988, 23f.

13. Elisabeth Schüssler-Fiorenza, 'The Twelve', in L. and A. Swidler, *Women Priests*, Paulist Press 1977, 117f.

14. Dietrich Bonhoeffer, *Letters and Papers from Prison*, The Enlarged Edition, SCM Press and Macmillan Publishing Company 1971, 370.

15. Elisabeth Moltmann-Wendel, *The Women around Jesus*, SCM Press and Crossroad Publishing Company 1982, 37f.

16. Anne Carr, *Transforming Grace. Christian Tradition and Women's Experience*, Harper and Row 1988.